SCEPTICISM

AND

HISTORICAL

KNOWLEDGE

STUDIES IN PHILOSOPHY

CONSULTING EDITOR
V. C. CHAPPELL
THE UNIVERSITY OF CHICAGO

SCEPTICISM

AND

HISTORICAL

KNOWLEDGE

JACK W. MEILAND

THE UNIVERSITY OF MICHIGAN

RANDOM HOUSE   NEW YORK

FOREWORD

This book is a study of a certain type of answer to the questions: "What is the nature of written history?" and "What is the nature of the historian's activities?" This type of answer has been given by, among others, some of the so-called "Idealists." I try to show that this answer can be rendered plausible by certain arguments for historical scepticism.

Thus, much of this book is concerned with a claim that is extremely paradoxical—the claim that, regardless of the amount of "evidence" available about the past and how that "evidence" is used by historians, historical knowledge is not possible, and hence the historian must be regarded as constructing or creating the past rather than as reporting the past. I call this view on the nature of written history "Constructionism." This view is often referred to or mentioned in writings on the philosophy of history. But it has not been discussed to any extent. Moreover, even those (such as Croce and Oakeshott) who hold this type of view provide little support for it. I believe that a much better case can be made for this type of view than has so far been made for it. My aim is to present the case for historical scepticism and for Constructionism as well as possible, so that both historical scepticism and Constructionism can be fairly evaluated. Historical scepticism may be incorrect and Constructionism may be unacceptable. But I claim that the arguments which I discuss in Parts IV and V of this book give these positions a good deal of plausibility. So, if these positions are incorrect or unacceptable, this must be proved, by, for example, showing that these arguments are not sound or that serious objections can be raised to Constructionism. If one or more of these arguments is sound and if there are no serious objections to Constructionism itself, then these positions on the nature of written history must be accepted even though they may be paradoxical. *Until these positions have been examined in this way, the commonly accepted view of written history will not rest on a firm foundation, for the central principle of that view—that historical knowledge is possible—will be unfounded.*

The discussion of historical scepticism is equally important because it necessitates examination of the basic concepts of history—those of "the past," "events," "evidence," "truth" and so on. The nature of written history can be understood only if it is understood what is involved in these concepts. Further, in examining these concepts, we examine certain assumptions which the historian commonly makes, for example, that there can be evidence about past events.

It might be said that if one or more of the arguments for historical scepticism is sound, this would only show that we must assume that historical knowledge is possible in the sense of proceeding as if such knowledge were possible. If it is true that we must assume this, then the discussion in this book will have shown something very important about written history, namely that this assumption must be made. But it is not true that we must make this assumption if there is another view of written history which does not involve the principle that knowledge of past events on the basis of evidence is possible. Constructionism is just such another view.

If Constructionism is correct, that is, if a generally accepted historical account is "a fable agreed upon," recognition of this fact may or may not lead to changes in historians' techniques or in the criteria of evaluation of written histories; but it will not change the world or the nonhistorical activities of people in the world. Recognition of this fact will give us a better understanding of what the world, or that part of it called "written history," is like. And if Constructionism is ultimately shown not to be correct, the discussion of this view and of the arguments which are used to support it will itself give us a better understanding of the nature of written history. *Thus, in either case, much can be learned about written history from an examination of Constructionism and of the sceptic's position.* This book, then, is an inquiry into the nature of written history.

Works by Croce, Collingwood, Berlin, and Nagel herein discussed are to be found in excerpted form in Patrick Gardiner's collection of readings, *Theories of History*; footnote references are given to both the original work and, where applicable, to Gardiner's volume.

I wish to thank Vere Chappell who read the whole manuscript and made many helpful comments on it. I also wish to thank William P. Alston, Arthur Burks, and Alan Donagan, who made helpful comments on earlier versions of chapters or parts of chapters.

CONTENTS

Introduction: Scepticism and the Nature of the Historian's Activities   *3*

PART I   *11*

CHAPTER

1   Croce: Documents, Interests, and History   *13*

PART II   *39*

2   Oakeshott: Is History Concerned with Past Events?   *41*
3   Collingwood: Can the Past Be Present?   *63*

PART III   *83*

4   Historical Relativism I   *85*
5   Historical Relativism II   *101*

PART IV   *111*

6   Correlation and Evidence   *113*
7   The Justification of Memory Beliefs   *121*
8   Verification and Meaningfulness   *142*
9   The Concept of the Past   *155*
10   Can the Past Change?   *173*

PART V   *187*

11   The Construction Theory of History   *189*

Notes   *201*
Selected Bibliography   *205*
Index   *207*

SCEPTICISM

AND

HISTORICAL

KNOWLEDGE

INTRODUCTION

᠊᠊᠊᠊᠊᠊᠊᠊᠊᠊

SCEPTICISM AND THE NATURE
OF THE HISTORIAN'S ACTIVITIES

The theories of history of the so-called "Idealist" philosophers of history have received little attention in recent years. Yet these theories of history are certainly the most interesting of all that have been presented. Moreover, the Idealists' theories are extremely important because they deal with fundamental issues concerning the nature of the historian's activities. In this book I discuss the general theory of history that some Idealists (and other philosophers) have held; I call it the "Construction Theory of History." The theories of at least some of the Idealists can be correctly understood only as Constructionist theories. I wish to show that the Constructionist position can be given considerable support and that it therefore deserves much consideration and discussion—far more than it has thus far received.

Each of the questions "Is historical knowledge possible?" and "What is the nature of the historian's activities?" is vitally important in itself. But there is a certain relation between the topics these questions embody. If the answer to the first question is that historical knowledge is not possible, we may find that this answer provides a good reason for adopting a certain view of the nature of written history. (In this book, the term "history" will be used to refer to written history or to the historian's activities, not to the course of past events.) Some philosophers of history have thought that arguments for scepticism about historical knowledge, that is, for the thesis that historical knowledge is not possible, provide a good, if not conclusive, reason for

adopting the Construction Theory of History and for rejecting a position that I will call the "Discovery Theory of
History." The Discovery Theory of History is the theory
that the goal of the historian is the discovery of facts about
past events, institutions, trends, and so on. The Construction Theory of History denies that this is the historian's
goal and asserts that the historian constructs accounts of
ostensibly past happenings for certain other purposes—it
asserts that the historian constructs or creates parts of the
past. In this introduction, I shall first explain what I mean
by the expression "scepticism about historical knowledge."
Then I shall discuss Constructionism and its relation to
scepticism, this being the main topic of this book. Finally,
I shall explain the plan of this book.

The position which I call "scepticism about historical
knowledge" or "historical scepticism" denies the possibility
of having historical knowledge, that is, of having knowledge
of the past on the basis of evidence about the past. There
are, perhaps, other positions that could also have this title.
For example, one who asserts that no historian *in fact* has
any knowledge about the past might be called a sceptic
about historical knowedge. But the sceptic's position discussed herein is far stronger than this. This sceptic asserts
not only that no historian *does* have knowledge of the past,
but also that no historian *can* have knowledge of the past.
He claims that historical knowledge is impossible.

This claim by the sceptic is not one that can be refuted
by an advance in the science of history. If the sceptic is
right, historical knowledge will not become possible when
historians become better historians or when they have collected more evidence or developed completely new historical techniques. For the sceptic claims that historical
knowledge is impossible in virtue of what historical knowledge would be or in virtue of the nature of the past or the
nature of evidence. And no advance in the science of history
can change the nature of historical knowledge, the nature
of the past, or the nature of evidence. Man cannot now
travel to other planets; however, this technological impossi-

bility will disappear if and when new techniques are developed. But, if the sceptic is correct, no "break-throughs" can occur in history such that historical knowledge will some day be possible.

It will probably be readily agreed by most people that certain aspects and events of the past will never be known because we will never have the documents, ruins, artifacts and so on, that could serve as evidence about those aspects and events. But this type of scepticism about historical knowledge bears little resemblance to the type discussed in this book; the type discussed in this book is far more radical than that just described. For if any one of the arguments for scepticism given in Part IV is sound, then there can be no historical knowledge at all about any aspect of, or event in the past, even if innumerable documents, artifacts and ruins are available.

That historical knowledge is impossible is the sceptic's conclusion. As I will show, he can give many different kinds of arguments for this conclusion. For example, he can try to prove that nothing can possibly serve as evidence about the past. It follows immediately from this proposition that there can be no historical knowledge, because *historical* knowledge is knowledge of the past based on evidence about the past. Even if there can be evidence about the past, the sceptic can try to show that the historian cannot make proper use of this evidence because he is biased in one way or another. The sceptic can try to show that there is no past about which one can know. He can try to prove that past-tense propositions (of which historical propositions are one species) cannot be meaningful even though they seem to be meaningful. If the sceptic can establish any one of these conclusions, he will have proved that historical knowledge is impossible. He will have disproved one or more assumptions commonly made by historians, on each of which depends the possibility of knowing about the past.

The topic of historical scepticism is important in its own right. To show this, let us consider an analogy to a situation in mathematics. Mathematicians have assumed, until fairly recently, that every true mathematical proposition can be given a proof within mathematics itself. Kurt Gödel proved that this is not the case. He proved that some true mathematical statements are not provable. Thus, he proved the impossibility of reaching a certain goal in mathematics, namely of proving every true mathematical statement. And this is an extremely important fact about mathematics. Similarly, in discussing historical scepticism we are investigating a certain possibility: the possibility of knowing about the past through the use of evidence. This is the possibility of having *any historical knowledge at all* about the past, not of knowing the past completely. The historian assumes that one can have such knowledge; the sceptic denies this possibility. If the sceptic is correct, he is stating an extremely important fact about history, analogous to, though perhaps more serious than, the fact about mathematics that was proved by Gödel.

The sceptic's challenge is equally important, furthermore, because in discussing it we must examine some of the historian's fundamental assumptions, as previously indicated. And in examining these assumptions, we will be investigating some of the central concepts in history and the philosophy of history. What do we mean by "the past"? What does it mean to say of a judgment that it is "objective" or "subjective"? What is an "event"? Unless we can answer these questions, we cannot claim to understand what history is.

The topic of historical scepticism is thus important in its own right. But this topic gains even greater importance from its relation to the question: "What is the nature of the historian's activities?" My purpose in this book is to examine one sort of argument—the argument from historical scepticism—for the Constructionist answer to this latter question. Briefly, the argument from historical scepticism is this: If it is impossible to have historical knowledge, that is, knowledge of the past on the basis of evidence, then the historian *should* be regarded as constructing accounts in the past tense which serve other purposes. This is not to say that if historical scepticism is correct, historians *must* be regarded as constructing or creating the past. Even if a person were convinced that historical knowledge is impossible, he could still regard historians as trying to discover facts about the past. Instead, what is claimed is that if historical knowledge is impossible, this constitutes a very good reason for adopting the Constructionist position.

Adoption of the Constructionist position may lead the historian to employ methods different from those which he now uses, though it need not do so. If the historian comes to believe that his goal should not be the discovery of facts about the past but, rather, the construction of accounts for certain other purposes, he may find that some new methods are more appropriate than those previously used. But he might instead find that the methods now used by historians are appropriate from a Constructionist point of view. The Constructionist position is thus not a position on what methods the historian ought to use. Instead, it is a position on *what the historian ought to be regarded as doing* when he uses any given method or set of methods.

The Constructionist position is not tied to any one philosophical position. Most philosophers of history—and, perhaps, all historians—seem to believe that the purpose of the historian is to discover facts about the past. But some philosophers of history have denied this. Croce and Oakeshott are two such philosophers of history; and by presenting what I consider to be the only plausible interpretations of their theories, I hope to show that their theories are Constructionist theories. I intend their theories to serve as particular examples of the Constructionist position. But although both Croce and Oakeshott are Idealists, it is not the case that Constructionism is a position which can be held only by Idealists. For other philosophers who are emphatically not Idealists have held views on history similar to those of Croce and Oakeshott. The pragmatist George

Herbert Mead is one, especially in his book *The Philosophy of the Present.*

The Construction Theory of History is admittedly extremely paradoxical; it will probably also seem very implausible and perhaps obviously unsatisfactory to many people. Yet I believe that a good deal of support can be provided for it by the type of arguments which I consider in Part IV. I do not claim that I have proved that theory to be correct; nor do I claim that it will ultimately be found to be correct. I claim that this theory can be shown, on the basis of arguments for historical scepticism, to have much more plausibility than might be supposed and that, since this theory deals with extremely important and fundamental issues in a plausible way, it deserves serious consideration and discussion.

In Parts I and II, I present interpretations of the theories of Croce and Oakeshott which show that they are Constructionists. I also try to show that they believed Constructionism to be based, at least partly, on historical scepticism. These two theories are intended to serve as particular examples of the general sort of theory with which I am concerned. In Part II, I also consider Collingwood's theory of history as an attempt to refute Oakeshott; I try to show that this attempt does not succeed and that neither scepticism nor Constructionism can be refuted in the way Collingwood tries to do so.

The argument for scepticism that has been discussed in recent philosophy of history is called "Historical Relativism." In the first chapter of Part III, several putative refutations of historical relativism that have recently been presented are discussed, in an attempt to show that they can be answered. But I believe that historical relativism does not in fact constitute a basis for historical scepticism; I try to show that it does not in the second chapter of Part III.

Since scepticism cannot be based on historical relativism, in Part IV we turn to a number of other arguments for scepticism. Each of these arguments purports to show that one or another of the necessary conditions of the possibility of historical knowledge is not fulfilled. If any *one* of these arguments is sound, then historical knowledge is impossible.

Finally, in Part V, I consider exactly how historical scepticism supports the Constructionist view. I then discuss the general features of that view (of which view Chapters One and Two have presented particular examples) and defend the view against a possible objection to it.

Thus, this book is a discussion of the Constructionist thesis about how the historian's activities should be regarded and of a certain type of argument that can be given in support of that thesis.

PART

I

In Part I of this book I give a certain interpretation of Benedetto Croce's philosophy of history. I wish to show that Croce's position on the nature of the historian's activities is a particular example of, or variety of, the Constructionist position. Thus, the discussion of Croce's philosophy of history will serve as an introduction to this sort of position on the nature of written history. Furthermore, it will serve as an example of the Constructionist position which is supported by the arguments of the sceptic. For Croce feels that he must adopt this position on the nature of written history partly because he believes that certain of these arguments for scepticism are sound. But he mentions only a few of the sceptic's arguments, and refers to even these only very briefly. In Part IV I try to show that at least five arguments can be given in support of scepticism about the possibility of historical knowledge. If these arguments are sound, they provide strong support for the Construction Theory of History.

It must be emphasized that I am giving an interpretation of Croce's theory of history. Some of the doctrines I claim that he held are not explicitly asserted by him and he does not explain the various parts of his theory in the ways in which I have explained them. But I believe that my interpretation is well supported by what he does say and that it does result in an important and consistent theory of history.

CHAPTER ONE

᠎᠎᠎᠎᠎᠎᠎᠎᠎᠎

CROCE: DOCUMENTS,
INTERESTS, AND HISTORY

Introduction

Benedetto Croce's philosophy of history is sometimes called an "Idealist philosophy of history."[1] Presumably it is called this because many of the characteristic doctrines of the Hegelians and the British Idealists (such as Bosanquet and Bradley) are expressed at various points of Croce's major work on history, *History: Its Theory and Practice*.[2] For example, Croce claims that each historical event can be understood only as part of an on-going process, that in fact each event can be fully understood only if the whole process is itself understood. We also find references to the Hegelian dialectic of opposites and to "abstract particulars" and "concrete universals" (these latter being outstanding features of Idealist logic). So it might seem that Croce's theory of history is based directly on these varieties of Idealism and that one will find his theory acceptable only if one finds these varieties of Idealism acceptable.

However, I believe that much of his philosophy of history can be understood, not as an outgrowth of Idealism, but as an attempt to take account of the sceptic's position, an attempt that is largely independent of Idealism. Further, I believe that Croce wished to have his theory evaluated apart from the truth or falsity of Idealism. Thus, although Idealism is no longer a widely held philosophical doctrine, Croce's theory of history, being largely independent of Idealism, still contains much of interest to us today.

It is apparent from several passages that Croce regarded his theory as at least partly an attempt to answer the sceptic. For example, he says:

For if the proof given has freed that concept [the concept of history] from one of the most insistent forms of historical scepticism (the scepticism that arises from the lack of reliability of "testimony"), it does not seem that it has been freed from or ever can be freed from that other form of scepticism, more properly termed "agnosticism," which does not absolutely deny the truth of history, but denies to it *complete* truth.[3]

I will try to show that Croce's theory does provide an answer to scepticism about "testimony" and to that form of scepticism known as "historical relativism." He certainly intended his theory to be an answer to the first; and his theory also, in fact, does provide an answer to the second.

Croce's answer to or refutation of scepticism is of the following kind: If history (in the sense of the writing of history or the activities of the historian) is regarded as being a certain type of activity, namely determining with certainty what happened in the past, then scepticism inevitably follows; but history should be regarded as a quite different sort of activity, namely as constructing the past; this latter view of history is preferable on two grounds: (i) it is correct as a theory of history, and (ii) it shows that scepticism can be answered. Thus, Croce answers scepticism by showing that history is a type of activity to which scepticism does not apply, not by showing that the sceptic's arguments are unsound. Croce admits that the sceptic's position does apply to written history on a certain theory of what written history is. But Croce maintains that the sceptic's theory of what history is is incorrect, and that scepticism does not apply to history on the correct theory of what history is. Croce believes that his own theory of history not only provides an answer to the sceptic, but it also is more correct than the other theories of history which he discusses.

What is meant by saying that one theory of history is more correct than another? A theory of history is correct if it describes and accounts for the various operations the historian performs. In doing so, it contains all or many of the distinctions that are usually made in philosophy of history, for instance the distinction between history and chronicle. All theories of history must admit that historians do certain things: they gather documents, they make use of facts, their results differ from the results of chroniclers, and so on.

But theories of history differ in their analysis of these central concepts. They differ over *what* "documents" are and *what* the relation between the historian and the documents is or should be, while agreeing that historians deal with documents. They may disagree on the *nature* of chronicle and on the *nature* of the difference between chronicle and history, while agreeing that chronicle does differ from history. Thus, theories of history are concerned primarily with an analysis of the central concepts of history, some of which are employed by historians themselves and some of which are used by philosophers in analyzing the nature of history. A theory of history which describes the facts about written history accurately and which provides an adequate analysis of the central concepts of history is more correct than one which does not do so.

Croce intended his theory to account for the basic facts about history, such as the difference between history and chronicle. He also intended his view to account for certain characteristics of history that are not taken into account by other theories, particularly in regard to the nature of facts and the nature of historical understanding. His theory is to be judged partly on the basis of how well it accounts for these facts about history. It is also to be judged on the basis of the adequacy of his analysis of the central concepts of history. In this chapter I want to show that his theory is best regarded as a Construction Theory of History and I want to show why he held this sort of theory.

"Every True History is Contemporary History"

The expression "contemporary history" is usually used to refer to the history of the very recent past. Croce's paradoxical dictum, "every true history is contemporary history,"[4] is intended to emphasize his view that anything deserving the name of "history" must be related to contemporary life. History is essentially related to what Croce calls "interests." "Past history" is history that is no longer related to interests; that is, it is not related to present interests but was related to past interests. A past history— for example, a narrative of the French Revolution—is not at first a history for the reader but a "document," that is, a piece of evidence. It is as much a piece of evidence for the *reader* as certain documents were for the *historian* who wrote the narrative. This book becomes a *history* for the reader when it becomes meaningful and significant for him—when it becomes part of his life. According to Croce: ". . . what were narratives and judgements before are now themselves facts, 'documents' to be interpreted and judged."[5] The same relation must exist between the historian and his documents. Just as the *cahiers* of the French Revolution constitute documents, which the historian interprets and out of which he creates history, so the narrative that the historian creates is a mere document or piece of evidence to his reader until his reader provides an interpretation of that narrative. And both the historian and his reader interpret their respective documents in terms of their interests. The reader uses the historian's narrative in the same way in which the historian uses the *cahiers*. By interpreting these two types of documents, the historian in the one case and the reader in the other determine the significance of the French Revolution. And in doing so, *each* creates history. History is contemporary because history exists only when it is created from documents by relating the documents to contemporary interests. Each may create a different history, just as two historians may give very different interpretations of the French Revolution. Different persons will find the French Revolution (as well as the documents and evidence pertaining to it) significant in different ways. This difference in interpretation is due to a difference in interests.

The distinction we commonly make between history and chronicle finds a place in Croce's view. This distinction is precisely the same as the distinction between contemporary history and past history. We usually regard a chronicle as a mere record of the facts in chronological sequence, whereas a history is the structuring of facts into a cohesive narrative and an interpretation of those facts with respect to the causes and significance of past events. But Croce points out that a chronicle is a *history* (in his sense of the term "history") *for the chronicler*. The chronicler did not include a record of every single event that occurred during the period covered by his chronicle. He selected certain events to record as being more important or more significant than other events during that period. And the selection that chronicler made was based on his interests; these interests are what led him to regard certain events as more important than others. The chronicle was a history *for him* because the chronicler's interests guided its creation. But the chronicle becomes a "mere chronicle" *for us* because we have different interests and do not find the list of events in the chronicle to be significant or important. For example, we may believe that the list does not give information about the sociological situation of the times or exhibit the religious or economic causes of various events, and we are interested in the economic, social, or religious aspects of the era. We do not now have the interests the chronicler had which, if we did have them, would render the chronicle a significant narrative of the era—that is to say, would render the chronicle a history for us.

This is how Croce's theory can account for the distinction between history and chronicle. "History is living chronicle, chronicle is dead history; history is contemporary history, chronicle is past history. . . ."[6] We do believe that chronicle and history are two different things. That Croce's view can account for this belief in the above way provides support for that view. Furthermore, although his distinction between history and chronicle differs from the distinction usually made between them, his distinction is superior to the usual one in some respects. The usual distinction is made in terms of form; a chronicle is a chronological record of events, whereas a history is far more than this. But Croce's distinction takes into account the fact that the chronicler does *not* record *every* event that happened in the time period with which he is concerned. The chronicler selects certain events to record and does not record others. Because Croce's theory takes this fact about chronicle into account, it seems a more adequate theory than the usual view of the nature of chronicle.

Further support for Croce's view is given by the occurrence of "revivals":

> For dead history revives, and past history again becomes present, as the development of life demands them. The Romans and the Greeks lay in their sepulchres, until awakened at the Renaissance by the new maturity of the European spirit. The primitive forms of civilization, so gross and so barbaric, lay forgotten or but little regarded, or misunderstood, until that new phase of the European spirit, which was known as Romanticism or Restoration, "sympathized" with them—that is to say, recognized them as its own proper present interest. Thus great tracts of history which are now chronicle for us, many documents now mute, will in their turn be traversed with new flashes of life and will speak again.[7]

Revivals of the sort represented by the Renaissance do not occur because, or only because, evidence and documents that were previously unavailable become available. Often the documents are already present and well known. Therefore, the cause of the revival must be some other factor. That factor is the presence of the proper interests.

Exactly what is the relation of interests to history for Croce? The above quotation indicates that certain parts of the past become significant because the historian has certain interests. Croce explicitly says this: ". . . for it is evident that only an interest in the life of the present can move one to investigate past fact."[8] But interests play a larger role than this. They not only lead the historian to investigate certain parts of the past rather than others, but they also guide his interpretation of those parts of the past. Croce seems to believe both that interests lead to the study of an era and that the era is interpreted in the light of those interests.

Croce may thus be seen as agreeing with Hegel's doctrine that spirit is the moving principle in the historical process. But Croce gives this doctrine a meaning quite different from the meaning it seems to have for Hegel. Hegel seems to regard spirit as the cause of history in the sense of being the cause of historical *events*. Croce believes that spirit is the cause of history in the sense of being an extremely influential factor in the creation of historical *narratives*. The human spirit is manifested partly in the interests it has. The history of the human spirit itself is partly a history of its interests. And interests determine to a large extent the nature and content of historical narratives. For this reason, written history is (at least in part) a history of the human spirit by being a manifestation of its interests.

Croce also says that facts "answer to" interests. "Therefore this past fact does not answer to a past interest, but to a present interest, in so far as it is unified with an interest of the present life."[9] What is this relation of "answering to" which obtains between facts and interests? Does Croce mean that the historian is presented with a range of facts by the documents (records, memoirs, chronicles, artifacts, buildings, and so on) and then selects those facts he finds important or relevant in view of his interests? It should be noted that this raises the problem of relativism or of bias in history. For on this picture of the historian's operations, the historian's standards, values, and interests would lead him to select certain facts rather than others as significant and to base his interpretation of the past on those selected facts. But this would result in an interpretation very different from one by another historian based on other facts. And the question then is: which interpretation is correct? If this is the view that Croce takes of the historian's activity, then his theory of history would be subject to the apparently serious difficulties denoted by the expression "historical relativism."

In fact, however, Croce rejects this view. He denies that the historian is presented with a group of facts and that the historian's first task is to select some of these facts as more significant than others. Croce denies this by denying that there are facts of the sort envisaged in this view. The facts envisaged may be called "brute facts." They are regarded by those who hold the view Croce rejects as the raw material of the historian. On this view the historian takes these facts as he finds them and fashions them into a history. His only operations on the facts are to select some of them and then relate those selected to one another. Croce rejects this view by rejecting the assumption that there are such "ready-made" facts. He says that ". . . those facts are a *presupposition* that has *not been proved.* . . ." And he doubts that a proof of the existence of "brute facts" can be given: "Having attempted the proof, we shall finally arrive at the conclusion that *those* facts really do not exist."[10]

Croce believes that facts are not *given* or *presented* to the historian but instead are *produced* or *created* by the interaction of interests with documents. He regards facts themselves as being "acts of the spirit," not as material presented ready-made to the historian.[11] According to him, it is ". . . the mind that thinks and constructs the fact."[12] Again, he talks about ". . . a creation of the unique fact, the fact thought."[13] Thus, for Croce facts are the end product of the historian's work, not its starting point.

In this way the historian's concern with facts does find a place in Croce's theory; he is able to account for the usual belief that facts are of crucial importance in history, just as he was able to account for the belief that history and chronicle are quite different. But just as he gave a different theory of the nature of chronicle, so he gives a different theory of the nature of facts. And in saying that facts are the result of interpretation of the documents in the light of interests, he seems to be denying that there is a distinction between fact and interpretation. If he is denying this, then he is not able to account for another usual belief, namely, that fact and interpretation are different and that interpretations are built on facts.

I believe that Croce *is* denying that this sort of difference between fact and interpretation exists. But Croce has good grounds for this denial. Croce seems to be pointing out that evidence does not come to the historian with a set of instructions about how it is to be used and what it is evidence for. The evidence is *taken* to be evidence for this or that; and taking it in this way involves a certain amount of interpretation. So Croce's thesis that documents are themselves interpreted and do not contain facts prior to this interpretation is warranted to that extent. Furthermore, if Croce defines "fact" as "interpretation of a single document," he can account for part of the distinction usually made between fact and interpretation in the following way: "interpretation" can be used to mean "interpretation of an era, a period, a movement, etc." and "fact" can be used to denote what we would call "interpretation of the individual document." Then interpretations would be based on facts, since interpretations of whole periods *are* based on interpretations of individual documents.

But Croce would still be partly incorrect in denying the existence of a certain kind of "brute fact." That a given document is discovered in this location rather than another, that it has a seal affixed to it, that it is handwritten rather than printed—all of these seem to be examples of "brute facts," that is to say, of facts that do not already involve interpretation. Of course, there is a sense in which *these* facts are not *historical* facts: they are not yet of

historical significance and will take on such significance
only in terms of some interpretation. Thus Croce is correct
if what he says is taken to be a denial of the existence of
brute *historical* facts. Historians do deal with the above
"brute" (nonhistorical) facts in their capacity as historians. They begin with these nonhistorical facts and use
them in making the documents "determinate," that is, in
creating historical facts. But *every historical* fact—even
such widely agreed upon facts as that Caesar crossed the
Rubicon or that Henry VII became king of England in
1485—is the result of interpretation.

Croce does discuss the distinction between historical
and nonhistorical facts. But he discusses this in terms of
documents because he is, at this point, still attacking the
view that documents themselves are historical facts. The
problem he considers is: ". . . how it is possible to avoid
going astray in the infinity of facts, and with what criterion it is possible to effect the separation of 'historical'
facts from 'those which are not worthy of history'."[14]
Croce does recognize the existence of the belief that some
"facts" are of no historical significance. Sometimes "general facts" are called historical and "individual facts" nonhistorical.[15] "Or, again, by historical facts are sometimes
meant those that treat of history proper, and by non-historical the stray references of chronicles. . . ."[16] Other distinctions made between historical and nonhistorical facts
are ". . . those between public and private facts, capital
and secondary documents, beautiful or ugly, significant or
insignificant monuments. . . ."[17] Croce believes that some
facts are regarded as historical and others as nonhistorical
because of the necessity of selecting from the infinity of
documents those that ought to be preserved for later
generations.

News, documents, and monuments are innumerable and to collect them all would not only be impossible, but contrary to the
ends themselves of culture, which, though aided in its work by
the moderate and even copious supply of such things, would be
hindered and suffocated by their exuberance, not to say infinity.[18]

Therefore some must be selected for preservation and others discarded:

And what is the logical criterion of this selection? There is none: no logical criterion can be named that shall determine what news or what documents are or are not useful and important. . . . The criterion is the choice itself, conditioned, like every economic act, by knowledge of the actual situation, and in this case by the practical and economic needs of a definite moment or epoch . . . the decision is always given from practical motives. . . . Now from this preserving or neglecting, in which our action is realized, is afterwards invented an *objective* quality, attributed to facts, which leads to their being spoken of as "facts that are worthy" and "facts that are not worthy of history". . . .[19]

Croce here seems to be saying that a document is preserved because it relates to some interest of the preserver at that moment. But documents that are not preserved could relate to some future interest and thus are potentially historically significant. Thus for Croce no document is, in itself, nonhistorical; all can have historical significance.

Documents and interests are constitutive of history, and both are equally important. There can be no history without documents.

Thus to talk of a history of which the documents are lacking would appear to be as extravagant as to talk of the existence of something as to which it is also affirmed that it is without one of the essential conditions of existence. A history without relation to the document would be an unverifiable history. . . .[20]

It is the relation to documents that serves to distinguish history from imaginative literature. History is a critical exposition of the document.[21] A history without documents, if it could be a history at all, would be similar to a past history, a history without significance for us.

It might be objected that while Croce claims that all of the documents must be taken into account in a work of history, this claim conflicts with his view that history is created by the interaction of interests and documents. For Croce's position on interests can be used, for example, by a historian to justify his not using a given document in his narrative: this historian can claim that the document in question does not answer to his interests. Thus, it might be said, Croce cannot claim *both* that written history depends to a great extent upon interests *and* that only those histories that are based on all of the available documents are "true" histories.

But Croce can reply that what answers to present interests is not the individual document but instead the whole era or period or some prominent aspect of the era or period being dealt with. This is shown by the use of revivals of *periods* as evidence for Croce's theory. Thus, Croce can still maintain that in dealing with a *period*, the historian must take account of *all* of the documents pertaining to that period.

Other Theories of History

What type of interpretation does Croce believe is to be given to documents by historians? This is to ask: What, according to Croce, should the activity of writing history consist in? In order to answer this question, we must first consider Croce's criticisms of other theories about what type of activity the writing of history can or should be. His own view is directed against these other theories and can perhaps be best understood in relation to them.

PHILOLOGICAL HISTORY

"Philological history" is the result of a theory which holds that history should consist merely in the compiling of documents. Croce says:

Chronicles that have been weeded, chopped up into fragments, recombined, rearranged, always remain nevertheless chronicles—that is to say, empty narratives; and documents that have been restored, reproduced, described, brought into line, remain documents—that is to say, silent things.[22]

This type of activity cannot qualify as history. History

consists in the interpretation of documents. But philological activity does not yield an understanding of documents and hence is, at most, a preface to history.

Philological history also leads inevitably to scepticism. By collecting and collating documents, by comparing them with one another to discover which is more authoritative and trustworthy, the philological historian hopes to discover the truth about the past. But he can never do so. This type of history is "intrinsically uncertain." One reason that it is uncertain is that

No "authorities" are certain while others are uncertain, but all are uncertain, varying in uncertainty in an extrinsic and conjectural manner. Who can guarantee himself against the false statement made by the usually diligent and trustworthy witness in a moment of distraction or of passion?[23]

This passage also shows that the problem of historical scepticism is one of Croce's main concerns.

POETICAL HISTORY

What Croce calls "Poetical history" substitutes emotions and purposes for interests:

Numerous examples of this kind of history are afforded by the affectionate biographies of persons much beloved and venerated and by the satirical biographies of the detested; patriotic histories . . .; that composed by the socialist, depicting the acts . . . of the capitalist; . . . Droysen giving expression to his lyrical aspiration toward the strong centralized state in his history of Macedonia, that Prussia of Hellas; Grote to his aspirations toward democratic institutions, as symbolized in Athens; Mommsen to those directed toward empire, as symbolized in Caesar . . .; Thierry celebrating the middle class in the history of the Third Estate represented by Jacques Bonhomme. . . .[24]

That is, this type of history has as its main function the expression of emotion. And the difficulty with this sort of history is that it treats the documents in a cavalier manner, thus rendering itself untrue. Historians of this stripe, ". . . with a view to obtaining artistic effects," are apt to mingle ". . . inventions with the data provided by the chronicles

and documents. . . ."[25] Aesthetic criteria are at the basis
of this sort of history because the poetic historian's purpose is not only to express certain emotions, but also to
produce those same emotions in his readers. This type of
activity, when it does not result in imaginative literature
(historical fiction being an extreme example), can easily
degenerate into propaganda. Thus everyone will agree that
poetical history is not history at all.

DETERMINISTIC HISTORY

The motto of the theory of history which results in
"Deterministic history" is "First collect the facts, then
connect them causally."[26] And this theory of history is,
according to Croce, wrong on both counts. As we have
seen, Croce denies that there are such things as "brute
facts" which need only to be "collected." Second, this type
of history involves an infinite regress:

But it is very well known what happens when one fact is linked
to another as its cause, forming a chain of causes and effects; we
thus inaugurate an infinite regression, and we never succeed in
finding the cause or causes to which we can finally attach the
chain that we have been so industriously putting together.[27]

Apparently Croce believes that even if x is causally related
to y, x is not the cause of y if x itself has a cause, say z,
for z is then the cause of both x and y. However, this is
not the way in which the term "cause" is ordinarily used,
and there seems to be little warrant for Croce's use of the
term. If Croce's criticism were sound, it would apply to
any causal theory, for example, a theory which asserted
that great individuals were the causes of historical events.

TELEOLOGICAL HISTORY

"Teleological history" also starts from "brute facts"
and purports to find an end or goal in the historical process: the production of goodness, of liberty, of commu-
nism, and so on. These brute facts are linked as steps in
the progress toward a final state, just as in determinism the

facts are linked causally. In addition to criticizing the notion of brute facts, Croce seems to believe that these goals and final states cannot be discovered merely by examining the documents themselves, and hence are inventions or fabrications imposed by the historian on the documents. These histories express the desire of the historian for the final state in question. And these elements of desire and fabrication show "teleological history" to be only a species of "poetic history."

The view that history is naturally divided into periods often stems from a teleological view of history or, at least, from the view that historical periods are stages in some sort of progress or development. Such doctrines may represent ". . . the history of nations as proceeding according to the stages of the development of the individual, of his psychological development, of the categories of the spirit . . ." and all commit the same error ". . . which is that of rendering periodization external and natural."[28]

These are the most important of the theories of history that Croce discusses and rejects. Each theory, as indicated above, is found to be mistaken for reasons that do not necessarily apply to the other theories. But I believe that there is a feature common to all these theories in virtue of which all are inadequate from Croce's point of view as theories of the nature of history. Each of them claims that the historian attempts to give an understanding of documents or facts by relating them to something else. The philological historian relates the document to other documents—he shows that a given document is consistent or inconsistent with other documents. The poetical historian relates the documents to some purpose of his own, for example to lead the reader to approve of democracy or imperialism. The deterministic historian relates a brute fact to other brute facts in a causal manner. The teleological historian relates each brute fact to some goal.

In rejecting all of these views of history, Croce is, I believe, rejecting the general doctrine that documents and facts can be understood by relating them to something *other than themselves*. He never states this explicitly, but he does sometimes strongly hint at such rejection. For example, he rejects periodizations of history which are "external."[29] And at one point he says:

> . . . in so far as we are such [historians] and really think in that way we shall not feel the necessity for having recourse either to the extrinsic bond of causes, historical determinism, or to that which is equally extrinsic of transcendental ends. . . . The fact historically thought has no cause and no end outside itself, but only in itself, coincident with its real qualities and with its qualitative reality.[30]

Passages such as these and the similarities among the theories of history that he rejects show, I believe, that Croce has a certain view of what constitutes historical understanding and historical thought. This view is different from the usual view of the nature of the historian's activities, just as are those of Oakeshott and Collingwood. When a document or a fact is related to something else, what is understood is not the document or fact itself but instead either its *relation* to that other thing or else the document or fact only insofar as it has this relation to that other thing. For example, to know that *x* is the cause of *y* is to know something about *y*, namely that *y* is related in a certain way to *x*. But this is not to understand *y* or to know the complete nature of *y*. It is only to know a certain and perhaps not essential aspect of *y*. The relations spoken of by the theories of history which Croce rejects are all what we might call "external" relations. They are not relations constitutive of the nature of the document or the fact; they are not "internal" relations in this sense. Instead, these relations are schemes or parts of schemes imposed on the document or on the fact from the outside. The document or the fact is supposed to fit into the already constructed scheme or system *and to take on historical significance or meaning through having a place in this scheme*. By being placed in this scheme (causal, teleological, poetical, and so on), the document or fact is given relations to other documents or facts. It is given historical significance by being given these relations. But as the scheme is imposed from the outside, the scheme, and hence the relations the document or fact has within the scheme, may not reflect the *internal character* or *nature* of the document or the fact.

Perhaps this view which is being attributed to Croce can be illustrated by what he says about "natural history," the history of the natural world. He claims that "natural history," or the history of nature, is not true history. Natural history proceeds by classification of the genus-species sort, according to Croce. To classify an animal or a geological formation as being of a certain type is to fit that individual into a scheme, a system of classification. The individual is thereby related to other individuals in terms of similarities. But this sort of procedure gives an understanding of the individual only insofar as that individual is similar to others. Yet what renders him an individual is just those features he does not share with others. So this sort of procedure can never give an understanding of the *individual's nature* as an individual. It can give an understanding of the individual only insofar as he is related to others by being regarded as an example of a certain type. Yet history is concerned with *internal nature* rather than *external relation*. Hence natural history is not true history. What Croce requires in true history is that the document or the fact be understood in itself, not as it is in relation to something else. The historian must understand the document in the sense of understanding its meaning or significance rather than, for example, its origins.

But what sort of significance—significance for or in relation to what? This is why Croce insists on the importance of interests in history. A document has significance (or is meaningful or important) for or in the light of the historian's interests. For example, the historian attempts to determine the sociological, religious, or economic significance of the document. This is not to impose an already created scheme on the document. Rather, the document becomes "determinate" or takes on a definite character in the light of interests. Croce seems to believe that to interpret a document is to give it a definite character *and* to assess its significance. These two activities are not independent of one another, according to him. A single document can be given many interpretations; it can have many kinds of significance or be seen to be significant in many ways. It thus takes on a determinate or definite nature when it is regarded in one way rather than in any of the other possible ways. The document is then called a "fact" by Croce. A fact is a significant document, a document that has a certain significance or importance in the light of some interest. This is only to say, as before, that facts involve a large measure of interpretation. Only after the facts are determined in this way are they to be related to one another. The scheme of their relations arises from the facts themselves. In other theories, the facts are regarded as given, as not involving interpretation, as already available; they are then related to one another in terms of a scheme or system that has already been adopted by the historian. In Croce's view, the facts are created by interpretation of the documents; then the system of relations into which they fit arises from their own nature. In this way the nature of the facts is exhibited rather than obscured by the scheme or system. As we will see in a later section, this difference between Croce's theory and other theories has important consequences for the problem of bias in history.

It is true that in Croce's view, documents and facts do have relations to something other than themselves, namely to interests. But these relations are not external relations. Each document is to be interpreted on the basis of that document's *own* properties in the light of interests, not by giving that document relations to other documents as, for example, a philological historian would do. And each fact is internally related to interests since that fact is a fact for a given historian because that historian has certain interests. The fact is what it is, partly because of those interests, not because it is regarded as given and then related to other facts. So although documents and facts are related to something other than themselves, namely interests, this relation is such that the historian is concerned, first and primarily, with the internal character or nature of the document or fact and only later with the relations it might have to other documents or facts.

The Nature of Interests

It is clear from what has been said that "interests" play a crucial role in Croce's theory of history. But what does Croce mean by the term "interests"? Thus far interests have been taken to be "the interests which a person has in certain aspects of civilization." For example, a person may be interested in sociology or religion or economics. As a historian he would interpret documents with respect to their sociological, religious, or economic significance. Polybius was interested in the effects of events on the fortunes of the Roman Empire, Augustine in the relation between Paganism and Christianity, and so on.[31] This interpretation of the term "interests" is the interpretation which renders Croce's theory of history most plausible and is the one that would be most likely to be accepted by present-day historians. But this interpretation is not the only possible one, and we must examine the others also.

At many points Croce suggests that the interests that are intrinsic to history are what we might call "practical interests" in the usual sense (not necessarily Croce's sense) of the term "practical." He says that history is such as to shed ". . . light upon an order of facts answering to a practical and ethical want."[32] He claims that the problem of which documents to preserve for the future is a "practical," not a "scientific" problem.[33] He emphasizes the importance in this connection of problems relating to one's future.[34] He stresses the utility of history.[35] The best evidence for this interpretation of the term "interests" is

his praise of Bolingbroke as a historian: "He then proceeds to paint a picture of those two centuries of history,
for the use, not of the curious and the erudite, but of
politicians."[36] All of this suggests that Croce believes that
the interest of the historian is in the gaining of practical
wisdom. The historian attempts to use documents pertaining to the past as a help in dealing with the present and the
future. He interprets documents in the light of present
practical problems. A view of the function of history similar to this is fairly widespread: history allows people to
avoid the mistakes of the past although it is not necessarily
engaged in for that purpose. But Croce may be going
even further. He may be saying that documents are to be
interpreted in such a way as to provide lessons for the
future or to aid in solving existing practical problems.

But there is another possible interpretation of what
Croce means by "interests." At several points he suggests
that history is the history of thought. In his Appendix I he
discusses several documents as documents in the history of
thought. He says:

Finally, whether the *De docta ignorantia* were written some time
earlier or later is something that may quite well be determined by
a different interpretation of this or that thought of Cusanus, but
it does not affect the function that the doctrine of the coincidence
of opposites exercises in the formation of logical science. Again,
whether the *Sepolori* was composed or planned prior to Foscolo's
visit to France would without doubt change to some extent our
representation of the gradual development of the soul and genius
of the poet, but it would hardly at all change our mode of
interpreting his great ode.[37]

According to this, the historian's interest is in the role of
the document in the history of thought.

Scepticism and Bias

Although Croce never explicitly states in what way
his theory of history provides an answer to scepticism, he

does state that his theory does provide such an answer. And I believe that we can determine on the basis of the foregoing discussion of his theory what his answer is. Croce's theory concerns the relation between the historian and the *documents*. Historians deal exclusively with documents (including memories); they never deal directly with past events. We have seen that Croce believes that the historian should attempt to understand each document and to ascertain its significance as it is in itself, not as it is in relation to something else. The historian should take documents as objects of interest *in their own right*. Documents exist in the present and by being interpreted in terms of the historian's present interests, the documents have value for the present. *The historian should be viewed as concerned with the contemporary significance of documents.* This theory is based, as I have tried to show, on Croce's views on the nature of historical facts, the nature of historical understanding, and the role of interests in the historian's activities. I now turn to the relation between this theory of history and scepticism about historical knowledge.

Croce believes that scepticism about historical knowledge is a sound position. He has previously been shown to believe that all "authorities are uncertain."[38] We have also referred (p. 14) to his belief that the reliability of testimony is questionable. He believes that if the historian is viewed as concerned with trying to bring his narrative into correspondence with past events, scepticism about historical knowledge is inevitable. For one can never know whether or not the narrative does correspond to past events. Croce believes that, in view of the intrinsic and inescapable uncertainty of history if history is viewed as an attempt to obtain certainty about the past, a different theory of history is required.

Croce's own theory is partly an attempt to provide a theory of history which does not lead to scepticism. According to Croce, the creation of history depends upon a certain relation between the historian and the documents. So, for example, any evaluation of the historian's narratives must be an evaluation pertaining to this relation rather than to the relation between the narrative and the past events in question: ". . . true history is that of which an interior verification is possible. . . ."[39] If the historian's activities are properly performed, his narrative is verified. Verification does not concern the relation of narratives to past events. This is not to say that historical narratives are not about past events. Such narratives are perhaps *about* past events rather than about documents; they perhaps refer to the past. But they are not to be judged on the basis of their correspondence (or lack thereof) to past events.

It is clear that scepticism about the unreliability of testimony, and in general about the relation between documents and past events, does not apply to Croce's position on the nature of history. For according to his position, documents are not regarded as being primarily testimony about the past. They are regarded as having present significance in their own right. This is the way in which Croce provides an answer to the sceptic. *The sceptic's position on the possibility of knowledge of past events does not apply to history when history is regarded as concerned with the present significance of documents, not with past events.*

There is another way in which the denial that history should be regarded as primarily concerned with past events is connected with Croce's view of historical understanding. As was said (pp. 27–31), the historian should be concerned with the *internal nature* of the document rather than with its *external relations*. Accordingly, Croce not only denies that documents should be related to external and imposed schemes (causal, poetical, and so on) but he also believes that these documents should not be regarded as related to past events, *for past events are external to and not essentially connected with or indicative of the internal character of each document.* Thus, Croce's view that the historian is not primarily concerned with past events is very closely related in this way to his rejection of the theories of history discussed earlier.

But if the historian is interested in the documents as documents in the history of thought, aren't those documents being regarded as a certain kind of testimony about the past? Croce gives his answer in the passage on the works of Cusanus and Foscolo quoted in the previous section. When a document is regarded as a document in the history of thought, what is important is the interpretation of the document. So-called "historical facts" about which the evidence can be misleading or unreliable—for example, the time at which the document was composed— would not affect the interpretation and significance of the document. Hence, even here, the historian does not require certainty about these "historical facts."

Croce explicitly intends his theory to provide an answer to this sort of scepticism. This sort of scepticism does not apply to history when history is viewed in Croce's way. But there is another sort of scepticism to which his theory can also provide an answer, though he does not explicitly say it *does* provide such an answer and he may not even have believed that it does. This type of scepticism is what was previously called "historical relativism." Briefly, it is this: every historian regards the documents or evidence from his own point of view; his values, standards, and interests greatly influence what he says about the past. As a result of these differences, different historians will give different interpretations of the past. Their "bias" will determine or influence their interpretation of the past. How, then, is it to be determined which, if any, of these different interpretations is correct?

Croce's answer to historical relativism also follows from his theory of the nature of history. His answer is based on a distinction between two types of bias, corresponding to two types of interests. We have seen that other theories of history attempt to impose on documents structures already created or to force documents into these structures, rather than first interpreting the documents—that is, first determining the facts. And in doing this these theories may well distort the documents. This is particularly true of "poetical history," history that has a propagandistic purpose. When a document is interpreted by relating it to other things, the document itself may be misrepresented. *This* sort of distortion, resulting from propagandistic and other interests, can be eliminated—in fact, it must be eliminated if history is to be created.

But not all interests, and hence not all bias, can be eliminated. As we have seen, Croce believes that the historian's interests are absolutely essential for the existence of history. To put it another way, the historian must have a point of view in order to use the documents. For there are no such things as "brute facts." Documents must be interpreted in order that there may be facts in the first place. Therefore, principles of interpretation are required. These principles in history are the historian's interests.

Thus Croce is saying that not all bias is invidious. The historian's primary concern should be with documents, not primarily with the past. Hence bias is to be regarded as invidious or not, depending on how that bias influences the relation between the historian and the documents, not on how it influences the relation between the historian and past events. Only that bias or those interests which lead to distortion of the *document* (rather than to distortion of the past) should be eliminated. Other sorts of interests not only should not be eliminated, but are absolutely essential to the creation of history. But, the Relativist may say, we still have the problem of determining which interpretation of the documents is the correct one. How are we to determine this? The answer Croce's theory gives to this question is that all interpretations conforming to the precepts previously discussed are "correct." Since history, according to Croce, does not aim at certain knowledge of a single past, there is no reason to say that only one interpretation is correct. All are correct, provided they "answer to some present interest" of the historian.

Has Croce Refuted the Sceptic?

The sceptic claims that knowledge about the past is unattainable, either because testimony is ultimately unreliable or because historians are biased (or for other reasons to be considered in Part IV). Croce has not denied this. Scepticism is answered by Croce by denying that historical narratives are to be judged on the basis of how closely they correspond to past events. He admits the force of the sceptic's position with respect to a certain theory of history and then develops another theory of history on the basis of which history is not affected by scepticism. Croce feels that his theory—that history consists in the construction of narratives that have contemporary significance—is the only plausible theory of history, partly because it describes more accurately the nature of facts and of historical understanding and gives a more adequate analysis of the central concepts of history, but also partly because it takes account of the soundness of the sceptic's position with respect to other theories of history. Yet Croce never tries to prove that scepticism about historical knowledge of past events is a sound position. In fact, he only briefly alludes to the sceptic's position. In the later parts of this book, I will try to show that scepticism can be defended and that this position does lend support to a type of theory of history of which Croce's is a particular example.

Croce claims that other theories of history are valueless because one can never *know* that a historical account does correctly represent a series of past events. Even if it is true that one cannot know this, it might still be possible to have justified belief—belief that has some probability—about past events. The historian may regard his account as probable, or even as very probable, even though he does not regard it as absolutely certain. Hence Croce may be unjustified in claiming that other theories of history must represent historians as aiming at certainty. They may aim only at probability, and such probability may be possible. Therefore in Part IV I shall try to prove that one cannot have even probability about the past, let alone certainty. But Croce does not try to prove that probability about the past is not possible. And to that extent he is unjustified in rejecting theories of history which claim that historians aim at obtaining knowledge about past events.

Finally, we have seen how closely Croce's answer to Relativism is tied to his theory. He admits the inevitable influence of the historian's interests, but claims that this does not vitiate history because, on his theory, history does not aim at certain knowledge of the past. Thus, if one believes that history does aim at absolutely certain knowledge of past events, Croce's method of handling the problem of relativism will not be plausible. Partly for this reason I will discuss, in Chapter Five, a reply to the Relativist compatible with the thesis that the historian aims at knowledge of the past. I will try to show that relativism is mistaken in a certain crucial respect and, therefore, does not present a problem regardless of what theory of history one holds.

What has been said in this chapter shows, I believe, that Croce's theory is an example of the Construction Theory of History. Croce believes that the historian should be viewed as creating the past through interpretation of documents in the light of his interests, rather than as discovering facts about past events through use of the documents as evidence.

PART

II

Michael Oakeshott's theory of history may be regarded as a Construction Theory of History. Furthermore, like Croce's theory, it is also supported partly by the use of an argument for historical scepticism. Thus, this theory serves as another example of the sort of position I wish to defend. I shall try to show that Oakeshott's position can be made plausible, even though it has a number of questionable aspects. R. G. Collingwood regarded Oakeshott's views on history as very important; in fact he called them ". . . the high-water mark of English thought upon history. . . ." Nevertheless, Collingwood believed Oakeshott's theory of history to be mistaken and regarded his own theory as proving that it was. I will try to show that Collingwood does not succeed in refuting Oakeshott.

Again, I want to emphasize that I am giving interpretations of both Oakeshott's and Collingwood's views. The arguments Oakeshott gives for his position are often not plausible. Accordingly, I have tried to give arguments for his position that are much more plausible. The same is true to a lesser extent in the chapter on Collingwood.

Thus, Part II is intended to illustrate further and to support the Construction Theory of History. I intend in Part II to render Oakeshott's particular version of this theory plausible and to show that it cannot be refuted in the way in which Collingwood attempts to refute it.

CHAPTER TWO

๒๒๒๒๒๒๒๒๒๒

OAKESHOTT: IS HISTORY CONCERNED WITH PAST EVENTS?

Introduction

Michael Oakeshott's theory of history as presented in his book *Experience and Its Modes* is admittedly based on Hegelian and British Idealism. But, like Croce's position, it can be regarded as independent of Idealism. First I will give several arguments for Oakeshott's position and will describe the theory of history that is intended to be supported by those arguments. Then I will discuss some objections to his position.

"All History is Contemporary"

Oakeshott agrees with Croce's dictum that all history is contemporary history, but gives this dictum quite a different interpretation from Croce's. For Croce it means that the historian's interpretation of the documents is determined by his present or contemporary interests. But Oakeshott denies that history is contemporary in the sense that contemporary interests determine what the historian will say about the past.[1] History is contemporary for quite a different reason, namely that it cannot be concerned with " . . . a world of past events to be discovered, unearthed, recaptured."[2] He says:

. . . history cannot be "the course of events" independent of our experience of it, because there is nothing independent of our experience—neither event nor fact, neither past nor future. . . . An event independent of experience, "objective" in the sense of being untouched by thought or judgement, would be an unknowable; it would be neither fact nor true nor false, but a non-entity. . . . The distinction between history as it happened (the course of events) and history as it is thought, the distinction between history itself and merely experienced history, must go; it is not merely false, it is meaningless. The historian's business is not to discover, to recapture, or even to interpret; it is to *create* and *construct*. Interpretation and discovery imply something independent of experience, and there is nothing independent of experience.[3] [Italics added.]

(This passage shows that Oakeshott's view on history is a Constructionist theory.)

Oakeshott denies that there is an inaccessible series of events called "past events" to be known about. It is not that history merely should be concerned with something else rather than with past events. History *cannot* be concerned with unobservable past events, for there are no such past events with which it *could* be concerned. We saw in Chapter One that Croce also denies that history is concerned with past events. But he never denies that there *are* past events. History, for Croce, should concern the relation between the historian and the documents rather than the relation between documents and past events, partly because one cannot have certainty about the latter relation. But he never denies that the latter relation exists. And because he does not deny this, Croce is perhaps open to the charge that he arbitrarily shifts the subject matter of history from past events to documents merely in order to answer the sceptic. This may seem like an *ad hoc* device since, it might be said, there are *still* past events that must be dealt with in one way or another. But although Oakeshott also denies that history should be regarded as concerned with past events, he is not open to this charge of arbitrarily redefining the term "history" because he gives a good reason why history should not be regarded as concerned with the past: there is no past for history or any other discipline to be concerned with. It is not that the term "history" *can* be redefined; rather, that term *must* be redefined. A Constructionist theory need not say that there are no past events in order to avoid the charge that can perhaps be brought against Croce's view. Such a theory could say that the past cannot be dealt with in *any* way if it cannot be dealt with in a historical manner. But Oakeshott avoids this charge by claiming that there are no past events.

Why does Oakeshott say that there are no past events or, alternatively, that past events are unreal? He claims that they are events that can never be experienced. But judgments can be made only about that which can be experienced. Therefore, judgments cannot be made about past events. And if judgments cannot be made about such events, such events are unknowable. For whatever can be known must have a definite nature or definite properties in order to be knowable and only things about which judgments can be made can have a definite nature or definite properties. Hence, nothing can be known about past events. This is apparently what Oakeshott means when he says: "An event independent of experience, 'objective' in the sense of being untouched by thought or judgment, would be an unknowable. . . ."[4]

Something unknowable—which not merely is not known but moreover cannot be known—is unreal: " . . . it would be neither fact nor true nor false, but a nonentity. . . ."[5] An analogy may be drawn here to "the ether," postulated by physicists in the late nineteenth and early twentieth centuries. The ether was an unobservable fluid consisting of exceedingly minute particles; the ether supposedly filled all empty places in space, that is, places in which there was no other matter. Its presence ruled out "action at a distance," for one body affected another by transmitting its influence through the ether. But the ether was unobservable. Experiments designed to show the presence of the ether did not do so. The ether was therefore held to be unreal or nonexistent. As Oakeshott might put it, the ether does not enter into man's experience in any way and, therefore, is unreal. Similarly, past events do not enter into man's experience in any way; only so-called "evidence" for those events does enter into experience; hence those events are unreal.

The kind of argument Oakeshott gives for this conclusion can be further explicated by discussing his theory of sensations. It has often been said that all knowledge is built on a foundation of sensations. One receives certain sensations ready made; that is, sensations—"red," "round," "tangy," "sweet," and so on—already are what they are and are presented as such to the knower. These sensations already have natures or definite properties. The knower operates with the given sensations to form judgments about the external world. But he does not operate *on* the sensations themselves; he has to operate *with* them as they are when they are given to him. According to this theory, there is a distinction between sensation and judgment. Sensations are presented to the knower prior to judgments by the knower; judgments consist partly of operations on ready-made sensations. Thus, sensations are both distinct from and logically prior to judgments. Oakeshott rejects this theory of sensations. He says that independent sensations (that is, sensations separated from judgment) are "inexpressible, unsharable, and impossible of repetition."[6] Such sensations are "utterly indeterminate." And because they are indeterminate—because they have no determinate or definite nature apart from thought and judgment about them, since (according to Oakeshott) thought and judgment endow them with a definite nature —such sensations can play no role in human experience. To be determinate is to have definite properties. Sensations are rendered determinate by having judgments of the form "*x* has the property ϕ" made about them, that is, *by having properties attributed to them through having judgments made about them*. Only after the sensation is rendered *determinate*—only after it becomes or is regarded as *this sort of thing rather than that sort, as having these properties rather than those*—can it be experienced or be a part of one's experience. Oakeshott would claim that one does not and cannot experience a sensation of, say, red apart from thought and judgment, because apart from thought and judgment that sensation is not *red*. In fact, apart from thought and judgment, it is not even a sensation. It *becomes* a sensation of red by being judged to be a sensation of red, that is, *by having a certain quality or property attributed to it through the making of a judgment*.

To say that a certain sensation is a sensation of red, or to regard it as a sensation of red, is to render the sensation "determinate." It is partly to classify the sensation as being similar to certain sensations and different from others. The object is given a definite nature or definite properties in this way; it comes to be regarded as having *these* properties *rather than* those properties. To say that one object possesses a certain property is to say that it is determinate with respect to that property—that the object does not both have and not have that property. It is partly to determine the nature of the object, for example, as having that property *rather than* not having it. Only determinate objects can play a role in human experience, because only objects that have had definite properties attributed to them can be experienced as *being of one kind or another*. No object that is experienced is ever of every kind or of no kind at all. It is always of one particular kind; it is determinate; it has definite properties. An object that is nothing, in the sense of having no determinate nature at all or of not being of any particular kind or of having no definite properties, is an object about which nothing can be said. Such an object cannot play a role in human experience; it cannot be related to other objects; its origins cannot be discovered, nor can its effects be picked out, for what is "it" which originated and has effects? When one knows about an object, what he knows about is its nature or its properties. Therefore it first must have a nature or properties before it can be known; that is, judgments must first be made about it before it can be known at all. Hence there are no such things as sensations which are "given," or presented ready made, and in that sense independent of and prior to judgment.

It might be objected that our judgments are not arbitrary. It is not entirely up to us what properties we attribute to objects. Objects do have properties before being judged. And these properties place restrictions on the judgments that can be made about those objects.

Oakeshott, however, could perhaps admit that what the objector maintains is true and still deny that it constitutes an objection to his position. For what Oakeshott should be viewed as maintaining is that only after definite properties have been attributed to the object can it take a place in one's experience; for example, only then can it be related to other objects. Only then will the object have a definite nature *for the knower*. The object may have a definite nature "in itself" prior to judgments about it. But prior to such judgments, it is not a definite and determinate object *for the knower*. It becomes a determinate object *for the knower* only after *he* makes judgments about it. Since it is then determinate for him, *he* can relate it to other objects, obtain knowledge about it—or, as Oakeshott might put it, the object then has a determinate role in *the knower's* "world of experience."

A very similar sort of argument can be given to show that past events are nonexistent. Objects acquire their natures—that is, come to be regarded in certain ways or come to be objects of that kind for us—through having judgments made about them, through similarities between them and other objects being noted, and so on. If the term "object" is used to denote that which has a definite nature *for a given person*, then "objects" (or, in Oakeshott's terminology, "entities") are created by being the subjects of judgments. They are given definite natures or properties by having those judgments made about them, that is, by having properties attributed to them. What are the conditions under which judgments can be made? The grammatical subject of the judgment (for instance, "the tallest boy in

[handwritten margin note: WHAT HE SHOULD HAVE SAID]

the class" in "the tallest boy in the class is wearing a red shirt") will refer to what the judgment is about. But grammatical subjects are of two sorts: demonstratives and descriptions. (Proper names can be construed as either demonstratives or abbreviations of descriptions.) If that which the judgment is about is *described*, then it is already taken to have a determinate nature because it *already* has those properties mentioned in the *description* of it. So this is not the sort of judgment by which something which has no determinate nature already can be given properties or a determinate nature, for this type of judgment (in which the grammatical subject is a *description*) presupposes that the subject matter of the judgment already has some properties (those mentioned in the description) and hence already has a partly determinate nature. This type of judgment can only make the subject matter *more* determinate by the attribution of further properties. But then how does anything come to have even a partly determinate nature if it does not already have one? The answer is that it receives a partly determinate nature through judgments that have *demonstratives* as their grammatical subjects. Such judgments have the forms "This is an *x*" and "That is *y*." *But such judgments require that their subject matter be present to the person who judges;* otherwise, he would not know what it is that the judgment was about, that is, what the terms "this" and "that" referred to.

But past events can never be present. Therefore judgments having demonstratives as their grammatical subjects *cannot* be made about past events. It follows from this that past events can never even begin to take on properties or a determinate nature. And if they cannot come to have a determinate nature, they are unknowable. But something unknowable can have no existence from the standpoint of human beings. Entities that are unknowable can play no role in human experience. It follows that past events can play no role in human experience. Thus, past events are nonexistent.

This argument purporting to show that past events are

nonexistent is not given by Oakeshott. But I believe that this argument is consonant with what he does say—it represents his point of view fairly and fits closely with his other arguments, particularly the argument concerning sensations—and it is a better argument than those he does give concerning past events.

Past Events as Related to the Present

Past events are nonexistent; they can play no role whatever in human knowledge. The above argument for this position is based on the thesis that past events cannot be present. But can we not know about past events by knowing about the evidence concerning them? Of course we cannot observe past events in the present. But such observation is not essential in order to have knowledge of the past, since we have evidence about the past.

In order to answer this objection, Oakeshott uses the argument of the sceptic, also cited by Croce. He says: ". . . it must always be impossible to ascertain the correspondence between the historian's world of ideas and the course of events which, *ex hypothesi,* is outside his experience."[7] And again:

. . . suppose "what really happened" to have some independent existence and suppose the task of the historian be to construct a present world of ideas to correspond to it, how is he to determine the correspondence? Apart from his present world of ideas, he can know nothing of "what really happened"; any correspondence he can establish, any comparison he can institute, must necessarily be confined within his present world. Immediately we think of history as the correspondence of the historian's ideas with "what was," historical experience becomes impossible, historical truth unattainable.[8]

Oakeshott uses this argument of the sceptic to support his position that " . . . the past is not 'there,' the same for all who consider it and from whatever standpoint they choose to consider it."[9]

What exactly is Oakeshott's argument here? That is, what use does he make of the sceptic's argument? He further says: "A fixed and finished past, a past divorced from and uninfluenced by the present, is a past divorced from evidence (for evidence is always present) and is consequently nothing and unknowable."[10] What type of "divorce" exists between the present and the past events in question? What Oakeshott may mean here is that since there is no way of determining whether or not any relation exists between present evidence and past events, it is not meaningful to talk of such a relation. It is not merely that one cannot know whether or not this relation exists. *Because* one *cannot* know whether or not this relation exists, statements about this supposed relation are meaningless. Such statements cannot play any role in human experience. Since they *cannot* be found to be either true or false, they are of no significance. They are meaningless. Since it is meaningless to talk of a relation between past and present, the past is "divorced" from the present. Statements about past events made on the basis of present evidence are meaningless because they depend on a presupposition—namely, that there is a relation between the past and present—which is itself meaningless. Consequently, statements about the past made on the basis of evidence cannot express knowledge about the past.

So the form of Oakeshott's argument thus far is this. He first attempts to show that past events are nonexistent. But his argument is open to the following objection: although the past cannot be present, it is still knowable because it is related to something that is present, namely, the evidence. So Oakeshott must also show that this relation between past events and present evidence is nonexistent and cannot exist, that all statements about such a relation are meaningless. This he attempts to do by citing the sceptic's argument that any statements about this supposed relation are unverifiable. Hence the sceptic's argument plays an extremely important—indeed, a crucial—role in Oakeshott's position.

The Meaning of Statements about the Past

If history cannot be concerned with past events because past events are nonexistent, with what *is* history concerned? Oakeshott says:

The fact is, then, that the past in history varies with the present, rests upon the present, is the present. "What really happened" (a fixed and finished course of events immune from change) as the end in history must, if history is to be rescued from nonentity, be replaced by "what the evidence obliges us to believe."[11]

All that history has is "the evidence," outside this lies nothing at all.[12]

There are not two worlds—the world of past happenings and the world of our present knowledge of those past events—there is only one world, and it is a world of present experience. The facts of history are present facts. And it is misleading to suggest that present facts are merely evidence for past events: historical events are facts, ideas in the world of the historian's experience, and there are no facts at all which are not present absolutely. *The historical past does not lie behind present evidence, it is the world which present evidence creates in the present*.[13] [Italics added.]

These passages show that, for Oakeshott, history is concerned with the present, not with the past as the past is usually thought of. This can be put in a different way: the past *is* the present for Oakeshott, or more specifically, the past is the present thought of or regarded in a certain way. Oakeshott is not denying that there is such a thing as the past or past events. He is denying that past events are past. He is redefining the expression "the past" to mean "the present regarded in a certain way." This position can also be stated as a thesis about the meaning of historical statements: historical statements are statements about the present. This does not mean that statements about the past are synonymous with statements about the present. A statement about the past *is* a statement about the present, and there may well be no *other* statement about the present with which it is synonymous. Statements about the past are not necessarily translatable into statements about the present; they *are* statements about the present, just as they stand.

That his position is ultimately a sceptical position and ultimately based on sceptical arguments concerning the possibility of knowing the past Oakeshott makes explicit:

And this is not a mere methodological scepticism; history is not merely obliged to *postulate* nothing beyond the evidence. What is beyond the evidence is actually unknowable, a non-entity. What is known in history is not "what was," "what really happened," of that we can know nothing; it is only and solely with "what the evidence obliges us to believe."[14]

Oakeshott is *not* saying that historians *need not* think of history as dealing with "the course of events." He is not saying that "the course of events" is dispensable. His position is of a far more sceptical sort, for he is saying that "the course of events" *must* be dispensed with, that it is not open to the historian to regard himself as detecting features of past events, because the expression "the course of events" is not even meaningful when intended in its usual sense. The historian cannot even *suppose* that he is dealing with past events *of that sort*, for such a supposition is not meaningful.

Oakeshott's Theory of History

If the historian's narratives cannot be judged by their correspondence with past events, on what basis can they be judged? Oakeshott's answer is: On the basis of their coherence. He seems to believe that historical narratives should be evaluated on the basis of how well their various parts "fit together," that is, how well the narrative expresses a coherent and unified view of the past. The parts of the narrative and the pieces of evidence are all present; any criterion which can apply to history must, in view of the preceding sections, be applicable only to that which is present; coherence is a criterion applicable to things that are present and that coexist with one another, and it is perhaps the only such criterion; therefore, historical narratives should be judged in terms of their coherence. Oakeshott's position here may be based partly on two facts about the operations of historians: (1) historians do try to "fit" new pieces of evidence into the interpretation they have made of the past; (2) if the new pieces of evidence cannot be fitted into that interpretation, often a completely different interpretation of the past is given which takes account of all of the evidence, new and old. Perhaps this is at least part of what Oakeshott means when he says:

. . . it is impossible to establish the truth of historical facts piecemeal. The truth of each fact depends on the truth of the world of facts to which it belongs, and the truths of the world of facts lie in the coherence of the facts which compose it. In historical experience, as in all other experience, there are no absolute data, nothing given which is immune from change . . . no single fact may be taken as historically true, and beyond the possibility of transformation, until the whole of the world of facts has achieved a condition of stable coherence. It is impossible, for example, to "fix" a text before we begin to interpret it. To "fix" a text involves an interpretation; the text is the interpretation and the interpretation is the text.[15]

Oakeshott thus denies that there are "brute facts," much as Croce does. "No distinction whatever can be allowed between the raw material of history and history itself, save a distinction of relative coherence."[16] What the historian begins with, rather than "brute facts," is a body of material lacking in coherence. His aim is to introduce a greater degree of coherence in that material by giving it a certain interpretation. And giving the material an interpretation may involve changes in the way in which the historian regards individual facts—a process which for Oakeshott (and Croce) amounts to changing those facts themselves.

Perhaps one reason why he believes that the criterion of coherence is applicable to history (and to all other forms of experience) is that he believes that all facts are related in the following way. When something is judged, it is brought under a certain concept—for instance, a sensation is brought under the concept of red by being judged to be red. This is to judge the sensation to be similar to others and to introduce a certain amount of what Oakeshott calls "coherence" into the "world" of sensations merely by "creating" that fact (the fact that that sensation is a sensation of red). It is to relate this sensation of red to other sensations. Thus facts have a certain amount of coherence just by virtue of being facts. The judgments which, so to speak, "create" the facts also introduce a certain amount of coherence into the set of facts by relating the objects of the judgments to one another. The task of the historian is to increase this amount of coherence.

Moreover, the criterion of coherence is a criterion of what the historian states to be a fact. This criterion determines what the historian regards as a fact. Earlier we saw that Oakeshott believes that history deals with "what the evidence obliges us to believe." How is it determined what the historian is obliged to believe? Oakeshott's answer is that the historian is obliged to believe whatever introduces a greater degree of coherence into his material or evidence. Since he is obliged to believe facts, it follows that a fact is that which gives greater coherence to this body of evidence. "Fact is what we are obliged to think, not because it corresponds with some outside world of existence, but because it is required for the coherence of the world of experience."[17] Since Oakeshott believes that in history "this proposition is true" can mean only "this proposition is what we are obliged to believe" (it cannot mean "this proposition corresponds to past events") and since coherence is the criterion of what we are obliged to believe, he takes coherence to be the criterion of truth in history.

But coherence is used as a criterion of truth in all areas of experience, according to Oakeshott. (The use of coherence in another area, that of the validation of memories, is discussed in Chapter Seven.) Hence its use in history does not serve to differentiate history from other disciplines.

What does differentiate history from other disciplines?
History is not different from some others in that it deals
with the past whereas they do not, for there are nonhistorical uses of the past. Some nonhistorical pasts are "the
remembered past," "the fancied past" (what might have
been), and "the practical past." An example of the practical past—the past as "designed to justify, to make valid
practical beliefs about the present and future, about the
world in general"—is the past as recounted in the Old
Testament. Here the recounting of the past is, according to
Oakeshott, ". . . an effort to make actual and impressive
their beliefs about their present world and about the character of God."[18] So, while Croce seems to allow the *historical* past to yield practical wisdom, Oakeshott appears to
deny this.

Moreover, Oakeshott denies that history can be defined
as the discipline that deals with unique events and persons
as unique because "what is absolutely singular is absolutely unknowable. . . ."[19] Oakeshott means by this that in
order to know something, that thing must be brought
under a concept by making a judgment, thus making the
thing in question similar to certain other things and hence
not *absolutely* unique.

History is to be distinguished from other activities by
what Oakeshott calls its "postulates." We have seen that
Oakeshott denies the existence of brute facts. Facts always
involve some amount of interpretation. Thus, principles of
interpretation are required. These principles cannot be discovered by inspecting past events or brute facts, for there
are neither past events nor brute facts. Since written history is created or constructed, the principles governing the
creation of history must be *brought to history* rather than
found in history after it is created. These principles are
imposed on the evidence; they are not discovered by use of
the evidence. History cannot show these postulates to be
true, for they are what make written history what it is in
the first place. These postulates govern the creation of

written history and thus are logically prior to history rather than shown to be true by history. And it is the use of *these* postulates rather than others that distinguishes history from other activities.

What are the postulates of history? First, there is what Oakeshott calls "pastness." Historical fact and historical truth ". . . are necessarily present . . . and at the same time they are conceived of in the form of the past."[20] Again: "The historical past is not a *part* of the real world, it is the whole of reality *sub specie praeteritorum*, it is the whole of reality subsumed under the category of the past."[21] Pastness is one category or postulate of history. The second category or way of viewing the subject matter of history concerns continuity and discontinuity. For example, historical individuals (events, persons, institutions) of the same type are distinguished from one another (sometimes arbitrarily in the case of events and institutions) by their beginnings and endings of existence. An individual from the standpoint of history is, so to speak, a temporal continuity of existence between two discontinuities. The third postulate or category is that of change. "And history, from our standpoint, may be taken to be the attempt to account rationally for historical change."[22]

These postulates determine or define a certain way of viewing the world. They define a point of view. "The world of history is, then, a past (though not merely a past) world of historical individuals, a world governed by the ideas of change, of continuity and discontinuity."[23] For Oakeshott history is a way of regarding certain objects and documents that are experienced in the present. History *is* the *present* as viewed according to these postulates or categories. This is what Oakeshott means by saying that history is reality "comprehended under the category of the past."[24] The historian creates and constructs the past out of the present. By regarding parts of the present in a certain way, the historian creates the past. Thus Oakeshott holds a version of the Construction Theory of History.

Is Oakeshott's Theory of History Satisfactory?

Let us now discuss some objections to Oakeshott's theory.

(1) W. H. Walsh raises the following objection:

> When it is said that our knowledge of the past must rest on evidence which is present that is one thing; but when the conclusion is drawn that the past *is* the present, that is quite another. Evidence for the past must no doubt be present in the sense of being presented to us now, but it does not follow from this that it must *refer to* present time, as it would have to if Mr. Oakeshott's conclusion were to be justified.[25]

Walsh is quite right that the proposition that evidence is present does not entail the proposition that evidence refers to the present. But this does not constitute an objection to Oakeshott's position, for Oakeshott does not claim that this entailment, as Walsh has stated it, does hold. Instead, Oakeshott claims that evidence must refer to the present, not primarily because the evidence is present, but mainly because there is nothing else that the evidence can refer to, since there are no past events in the usual sense of the expression "past events."

(2) But what does the term "evidence" mean for Oakeshott? One uses evidence when more direct methods of ascertaining the truth are not available. However, if something is evidence for *x* and *x* is present (as when Oakeshott maintains that evidence relates to past events and that past events are present), then why is evidence needed or used at all? One has a much more direct method than the use of evidence for finding out about things that are present, namely observing the present things themselves.

(3) It is possible that Oakeshott means that the (present) evidence *constitutes* the past events in some way—that when one regards the evidence in a certain way, one is regarding the *evidence* (which is present) as past. But then what is it that makes a present object a piece of evidence and another present object not a piece of evidence? As historians now regard the matter, an object

counts as evidence because of a relation that object is supposed to have to a past event. But if the evidence *is* the past event, it would have *this* relation to itself. Is this relation the sort of relation that something can have to itself? Or does Oakeshott mean that the present object viewed as evidence has a certain relation to that same object when viewed as part of a past event? But what would this relation be?

(4) In order to view the present as past, the historian must know what it is for an event or state of affairs to be past. That is, he must have the concept of the past. But how could he have acquired this concept? He cannot have acquired it by experiencing a past event, since Oakeshott claims that everything that is experienced is present. Nor could he have acquired it by being presented with a definition of the expression "past event," since there seems to be no such definition. Oakeshott would have to say that the concept of the past is an *a priori* concept. But then his theory becomes subject to any difficulties to which a theory of *a priori* concepts is subject. (The acquisition of the concept of the past will be discussed in Chapter Nine.)

(5) If the past is present as Oakeshott claims, then the past can change: the past will change when the present changes. It is not that the evidence for the past changes; the past itself changes. But can the past change? Is this allowed by our concept of the past? (This will be discussed further in Chapter Ten.)

(6) Even if the past can change, the following closely related problem arises. A proposition about a past event, such as the meeting of the National Assembly at Versailles, can be made at different times t_1 and t_2. And each time this proposition is uttered, it at least seems to be about the same subject matter. But, according to Oakeshott, each time it is uttered, that proposition is about something which is present. Hence that proposition will be about different things at t_1 and t_2 if there is a change in the relevant aspect of the present between t_1 and t_2. But if such a change takes place between t_1 and t_2, can the

proposition about the National Assembly have the same *meaning* at t_2 as it has at t_1? That is, can the same proposition even be expressed at t_2 if such a change takes place? Certainly it should be possible to express the same proposition at two different times. But if the present has changed, the proposition could not be about the same thing at t_2 as it was at t_1, and hence could not be the same proposition that was expressed at t_1.

Suppose that the proposition about the National Assembly is "really" about state of affairs S_1 at time t_1. Suppose also that S_1 goes out of existence between t_1 and t_2. If this proposition is to have the same meaning—if it is to assert the same thing as it did at t_1—it must be about the same thing. It was about S_1. But since S_1 no longer exists, it can no longer be about S_1. One might object here: why couldn't it still be about S_1, since, though S_1 no longer exists, it did exist at t_1? But if at t_2 the proposition were about S_1, that proposition would be about something which is past. Yet, according to Oakeshott, no proposition can be about something which is past, since there is nothing which is past. Hence that proposition could not be about the same thing at t_2 as it was at t_1, so it could not have the same meaning at t_2 as it does at t_1. Thus Oakeshott's theory seems to have the very paradoxical consequence that in some cases it is not possible to express a proposition at two different times. In particular, if the evidence about the National Assembly of 1789 changes between t_1 and t_2, it would not be possible to express the same proposition about the National Assembly at t_2 as one could at t_1.

Oakeshott might answer this by saying that the proposition may have been about different states of affairs at t_1 and t_2, but these states of affairs may have been states of affairs of the *same objects*. That is, he might deny that the present can change so that two successive states of affairs can be *completely* different. The proposition will be about the *same* objects at t_1 and t_2; this is why it can be said to be about the *same* past event. But then how could Oakeshott account for the possibility of having two completely different pieces of evidence for the same event? That is, how could he explain the possibility of two statements being about two *completely different* but simultaneous states of affairs (states of affairs of completely different objects) and yet both statements being about the same past event when he seems to be saying that statements about the past are statements about evidence? We certainly do make statements about the *same* past event on the basis of pieces of evidence which are *completely different* from one another. Oakeshott would say that these statements about past events are in fact about that evidence. But if these statements about the same past event are in fact about the evidence and if the pieces of evidence are *completely different*, then how can these two statements be about the *same* past event?

(7) I believe that Oakeshott would reply to (6) and several other of these objections in the following way: "These objections are objections to my theory only if my theory is interpreted as holding that the past is the present and that statements about the past are statements about the present. But this is not a correct interpretation of my position. I do not say that the past is the present. Instead, I say that the past is *the present viewed in a certain way*. And statements about the past are statements about *the present as viewed in a certain way*." How would this reply by Oaskeshott enable his theory to avoid these objections? Let us take (6) as an example. He could say: "Two different statements, each about a different piece of evidence, can be statements about the same past event because those two statements are statements about two different things each of which is viewed in the same way as the other." That is, it is *their being viewed in the same way* that makes statements about them statements about the same past event, even though they are also about different present objects and states of affairs.

Thus, the crucial question is: What does Oakeshott mean by "viewing a piece of evidence in a certain way"?

He might mean two things by this. (a) He might mean that each piece of evidence is regarded as being identical with a past event. But he cannot say this if he is to avoid objection (6); for if each piece of evidence or each present state of affairs is identical with some past event, then a statement about one piece of evidence cannot be about the same past event as a statement about a completely different piece of evidence because different pieces of evidence will be identical with different past events. If two pieces of evidence were identical with the same past event, they would be identical with one another, since if any two things are identical with the same thing, they are identical with one another. (b) He might mean that each of these pieces of evidence is viewed as being *related to* (as being evidence for) the same past event. But if Oakeshott says this, then historical statements will be either statements about the evidence, statements about the supposed relation between the evidence and the supposed past event, or statements about the past event. If such statements are about the evidence, then they are about different things (though not completely different things) and cannot be about the same thing (the same past event). And Oakeshott cannot say that he is talking about the supposed relation and the supposed past event, rather than the relation and the past event, for he would deny, as we have seen, that it is even *meaningful* to *suppose* that there are such past events and hence that it is meaningless to suppose that these past events have relations of any kind.

Oakeshott and Historical Scepticism

Like Croce, Oakeshott finds the essence of history in the relation between the historian and the present evidence, rather than in the relation between the historian and past events or between present evidence and past events. But Oakeshott's view is more extreme. He denies that there are past events in the usual sense of that expression. Thus, he denies the possibility of having historical knowledge in the usual sense of *that* expression. Oakeshott is a sceptic about historical knowledge if "historical knowledge" means "knowledge of this sort of past event."

But, one might say, Oakeshott is only a partial sceptic. He merely redefines the expression "past event." By "past event" he means "present state of affairs as viewed in a certain way, namely under the category of the past." And we can surely have knowledge of *this* sort of past event, since we can have knowledge about the present. So Oakeshott is perhaps not a sceptic after all, since given the appropriate senses of the expressions "past event" and "historical knowledge," Oakeshott does seem to affirm that one can have historical knowledge.

When I refer to "Oakeshott's position," I will be referring to that position as characterized above and in the previous sections. But Oakeshott himself would apparently not accept this characterization and interpretation of his position. For he seems to be sceptical about the possibility of historical knowledge in this new sense of "historical knowledge" too. He says of history that

. . . its form contradicts the nature of its content. . . . The world of historical fact, truth and reality appears to lie in the past; historical reality is a past reality, and the notion of the past cannot be dismissed from history without dismissing history itself. But to suppose this world of history actually to lie in the past, to accept it (that is) in the form in which it is satisfactory in historical experience, involves us in a radical contradiction. It obliges us to suppose a world which is not a world of ideas, to suppose facts which are not in experience, truths which are not true, reality which is not real. For no fact, truth or reality is, or can be, past. . . . The world seen under the category of the past is the world seen imperfectly. . . . Taken by itself, the world of history is abstract and defective from end to end; and only by abandoning it altogether shall we find ourselves once more on the way to a world of experience satisfactory in itself.[26]

Oakeshott is saying that even on his own theory, history involves a contradiction and hence cannot yield knowledge of any type of past at all. He claims to have proved that written history cannot give knowledge either about an independent course of past events or about the present (when the present is viewed as the past, as it must be viewed in history). The usual view of written history is that it deals with past events; but this view renders historical statements meaningless. His own view is that it deals with the present viewed in a certain way, namely as past; but he seems to believe that even his own view renders historical statements meaningless because it is not meaningful even to view anything as past or under the categories of history. Oakeshott might even say that all of the objections to his theory which I raised in the previous pages help to prove that historical knowledge is impossible even on his own theory. Although this may be Oakeshott's final position, he spends most of his time discussing the position described in the previous sections. That position is more defensible than is his final view—if there is a way of regarding parts of the present as past without also regarding them as "facts which are not in experience." Such a way would involve regarding present objects as neither present nor past (nor future) in the usual senses of those terms, but in some other, perhaps nontemporal, manner; and Oakeshott does not prove that there can be no such way of regarding objects which is also a way that could be called "historical." Such a way would, of course, involve a redefinition of the expressions "the past," "past events," and "written history."

Oakeshott and Constructionism

Like Croce, Oakeshott bases his position to a large extent on arguments for scepticism about the possibility of knowing about past events. And, again like Croce, he believes that if written history is meaningful at all, it is the result of creation and construction rather than of discovery and interpretation. The historian creates the historical past by regarding parts of the present in a certain way, a way that is determined by the criterion of coherence and by the categories of the past, of continuity and discontinuity, and of change.

CHAPTER THREE

𝕡𝕦𝕡𝕦𝕡𝕦𝕡𝕦𝕡𝕦𝕡

COLLINGWOOD: CAN THE
PAST BE PRESENT?

Collingwood and Oakeshott

R. G. Collingwood's theory of history is intended to answer scepticism about the possibility of historical knowledge. Collingwood often uses the term "the sceptic" to refer to those whom he is opposing. It is clear that the sceptic Collingwood is arguing against is either Oakeshott himself or a type of sceptic of which Oakeshott provides a typical example. In his book *The Idea of History* Collingwood discusses Oakeshott's views on history and says:

The historian, if he thinks that his past is a dead past, is certainly making a mistake; but Oakeshott supposes that there is no third alternative to the disjunction that the past is either a dead past or not past at all but simply present. The third alternative is that it should be a living past, a past which, because it was thought and not mere natural event, can be re-enacted in the present and in that re-enactment known as past. . . . So far as historical experience is thought, therefore, what it experiences or thinks as past is really past. The fact that it is also present does not prevent it from being past, any more than, when I perceive a distant object, where perceiving means not only sensation but thought, the fact that I perceive it here prevents it from being there.[1]

Collingwood thus attempts to answer the sceptic by holding both that all experience is in the present and that there are independent past events that can be experienced, and then reconciling these by saying that certain portions of the past can be past and present at the same time. Thus, the past can be known as something which is also present.

We have seen in Chapter Two that Oakeshott's scepticism is based on a variant of the following sort of argument: Since we cannot be directly acquainted with the
past, nothing can serve as evidence about past events; E
can be regarded as evidence for P if and only if E and P
have sometimes been found together: for example, the
presence of certain types of clouds can count as evidence
for the imminence of rain if and only if clouds of those
sorts have been found to be present prior to rain in previous cases; but this kind of procedure is impossible in the
case of the past because the past is unobservable and
hence the co-presence of the putative evidence and what it
is evidence for can never be observed; hence nothing can
serve as or be counted as evidence about happenings in the
past.

As we have seen, Collingwood's solution to this problem is to deny the premise that we cannot be directly
acquainted with the past. He claims that we can be directly acquainted with it or with a certain portion of it,
namely the intentions of past agents. Thus, evidence (in
the usual sense of "evidence") about the past is not necessary. Since we can have *direct* knowledge about the past,
we do not need *indirect* knowledge of the past of the sort
obtainable by the use of evidence. The sceptic's argument
shows only that we cannot have indirect knowledge of the
past. But, according to Collingwood, we do not need *indirect* knowledge of the past because we can have *direct*
knowledge of the past. So the sceptic's claim that we cannot have knowledge of the past is not correct. And we can
be *directly* acquainted with the past because a portion of
the past can be brought into the present and, so to speak,
"directly observed." This is what he means by the expression "re-enactment of past thought." Of course, if a part
of the past can be brought into the present, then the relation between historical evidence and what it is evidence for
must be regarded in a certain way, namely, consideration
of the evidence does not provide support for propositions
about the past but instead aids in the process of re-creating

the past. Evidence is not used, and should not be regarded as being used, in order to know indirectly about the past, as is usually thought by historians; instead, evidence is used, and should be regarded as being used, to bring the past into the present so that the past can be known directly.

On Collingwood's view, evidence is handled in just the way it is now handled by historians. Collingwood's view differs from the usual view, not in how the evidence is handled, but in what the evidence is used for or in how the results of the use of evidence should be regarded. According to Collingwood, the result of handling evidence in the way historians now do and in using all of the various historical techniques which are now being used is the bringing of the past into the present, not the providing of support for propositions about the past. So Collingwood is not advising the historian to use different techniques. He is advising the historian to view the results of using those same techniques in a different way, in order to answer the sceptic. Collingwood is saying that "re-enactment" of parts of the past is what historians in fact do.

Before discussing his arguments for the possibility of re-creating the past, let us first see in the next section why Collingwood believes that knowledge (through re-creation) of past intentions is the key element in knowledge of the past. Then, in the third section, I will discuss the arguments for Collingwood's claim that past intentions can be re-enacted and thus brought into the present. Finally, I will try to show that Collingwood's position is not satisfactory.

Intentions and Historical Knowledge

Knowledge of past intentions is regarded by Collingwood as being the key element in historical knowledge for the following reason:

For history, the object to be discovered is not the mere event, but the thought expressed in it. To discover that thought is already to understand it. After the historian has ascertained the facts, there is no further process of inquiring into their causes. When he knows what happened, he already knows why it happened.[2]

Collingwood is claiming here that to know what the agent's intentions are is to know both *what* the agent is doing and *why* he is doing it. Let us consider the case of a man who is digging a hole in the ground. We ask him *what* he is doing. We might have instead asked him the same question in the following forms: "*What* are you digging that hole for?" or "*Why* are you digging that hole?" We are asking what his aim in digging that hole is or what the intention is with which he is digging that hole. He might answer: "I am digging a hole in order to plant a tree." His purpose or intention is to plant a tree, and so he can say: "In order to plant a tree" in answer to our question: "*Why* are you doing that?" But it must be emphasized that we asked *exactly* the same question by asking: "*What* are you doing?" And the person could have replied: "I am planting a tree." This description "planting a tree" is a description of his action—of *what* he is doing. Yet it is what we might call a description of his action in terms of his intention (to plant a tree). Hence when he describes what he is doing as "planting a tree," *what* he is doing is being described in terms of or in relation to what he intends. So we can know *what* he is doing by knowing what his *intention* is. And, as the above example shows, if we know what his intention is, then we also know *why* he is doing what he is doing. This is possibly the reason why Collingwood said of purposive actions that to know (by knowing what the agent's intention is) *what* action it is is to know *why* that action was done.[3]

But if this is what Collingwood means by this dictum, then the dictum is misleading, if not wholly incorrect. The dictum is: when the historian knows what happened, he already knows why it happened. It would seem that the phrase "what happened" refers to the same thing that the term "it" in "why it happened" stands for. That is, it would seem that the dictum is about one action—that to know the agent's intention is to know what that one action is and why he is performing that one action. But in the example given above, what action is that one action? Is it the digging of the hole or the planting of the tree? In the example there are surely two actions involved: the digging and the planting. In knowing the agent's intention, we know *what* he is doing, namely planting a tree. But this does not tell us *why* he is planting a tree; it tells us why he is digging a hole. So when we know *what* he is doing, we know about one action (planting a tree) and when we know *why* he is doing it, we know about another action (digging a hole). And, contrary to what Collingwood's dictum strongly implies, there *is* something more to be known of the "why" variety, namely, *why* he is planting a tree.

There are several replies that Collingwood might make to this. (1) He might deny that "digging a hole" and "planting a tree" are two actions, since after all the former is closely related to the latter and is in fact part of doing the latter. Still, if the agent never reached the stage of putting the tree into the ground, he would still be said to have dug the hole, and this is evidence for the view that digging the hole is, even in this example, a distinct action from planting a tree. One may perform one action in the course of performing another, but they are still different actions. (2) Collingwood might say that in order to have the kind of knowledge he is talking about, we must know *all* of the agent's intentions in performing that action. Then we would also know why the agent was planting a tree.

Several things must be said here. First, the reason why the agent is planting a tree may have nothing to do with further *intentions* of the agent. For example, he may be planting a tree purely for the pleasure he finds in planting trees. But the pleasure is not some further thing he intends to produce. Second, there may be intentions of the agent that explain why he performed a certain action, but that cannot be used to characterize what he is doing. For example, if the agent distributed campaign literature for a certain Senator because he felt that the Senator would help to bring about world peace, even if we could say: "He (the agent) intends that there should be world peace," we could not say: "He is trying to bring about world peace." So it is not clear that the equating of "knowing what" and "knowing why" will hold for all or most intentions of the agent. Moreover, if one can know what action the agent is performing in some way other than knowing what his intention is, it may not always be true that to know what the action is is to know why the agent performed that action. Even if Collingwood's dictum is not misleading in the way previously indicated, these qualifications greatly reduce its significance for the philosophy of history.

It is possible that Collingwood meant something else by this dictum. Collingwood says that every action has an "outside" and an "inside," the "outside" being everything about the event which can be described in terms of bodies and their movements and the "inside" being everything about the event which can be described in terms of thought.[4] So his dictum might mean: when one knows what action was performed, one knows the intention with which it was performed; for if one did not know that intention, one would not know the "inside" of that action and therefore would not know completely what action had been performed. Only past events which have "insides" can be dealt with by the historian, presumably because only they have parts or aspects which can be present as well as past.

Perhaps one other reason why Collingwood emphasized this dictum, and thus the role of intentions in history, is that intentions provide a linkage or interconnection among events, that is, a connection between what the agent does at one moment and what he does at a later moment (similar to the connection between digging a hole and planting a tree). Such connections are, of course, extremely important in historical explanations of past actions. This is perhaps why Collingwood often uses the term "plan" in discussing intentions. The term "plan" suggests an intention that is complex in the sense that several actions are involved in realizing the intended state of affairs. Thus, intentions of the sort called "plans" can give coherence and structure to a series of past actions by relating them to one another within the plan or as different parts of the same plan.

Can Past Intentions Be Re-enacted?

Having considered what argument Collingwood might have given for his belief that historical knowledge consists primarily in knowledge of the intentions involved in past events, let us next consider the argument Collingwood does give for his position that past intentions can be re-enacted by the historian. The claim that past intentions can be re-enacted not only would, if true, show the sceptic to be incorrect, but also is the foundation of Collingwood's theory of history, that is, of his theory of the nature of the historian's activities. Consequently, his argument for this claim must be discussed.

An intention is a thought or an act of thought, according to Collingwood. So Collingwood first considers the characteristics of acts of thought in general. Can any act of thought be re-enacted? Suppose that Euclid thinks or asserts: "The base angles of an isosceles triangle are equal," and suppose that at a much later time Collingwood also thinks this or asserts this. Collingwood's opponent would say that Euclid's act of thought is a different act of thought from Collingwood's. Collingwood states his opponent's position in the following way:

. . . the truth which I recognize, or the proposition which I assert, is the same truth which Euclid recognized, the same proposition which he asserted. But my act of asserting it is not the same act as his; that is sufficiently proved by either of the two facts that they are done by different persons and are done at different times. My act of apprehending the equality of the angles is therefore not a revival of his act, but the performance of another act of the same kind. . . .

On this view, the relation between my act of now thinking "the angles are equal" and my act of thinking it five minutes ago is a relation of numerical difference and specific identity. The two acts are different acts but acts of the same kind.[5]

The opponent would admit that these two acts are the same in a certain respect, namely that the same proposition was thought or asserted in each case. But the two acts were still different acts, much as two freshly minted quarters might have exactly the same properties, that is, might be exactly the same in every respect (except spatial and temporal location), and yet are two different quarters. Collingwood expresses this position by saying that *the two acts* (or the two quarters) *are specifically the same* (or *exactly similar*) *but numerically different.* But since the two acts of thought are numerically different, one is not the re-enactment of the first. Collingwood's act of thought is exactly similar to Euclid's act of thought in every respect, but they are still different acts because one occurs at a different time from the other. And since they are two different acts, Collingwood's act of thought cannot be the re-enactment of Euclid's act. Collingwood's act cannot be, so to speak, the resurrection of Euclid's act. It can be *exactly similar* to Euclid's act, but it cannot be *numerically identical* with Euclid's act. Thus it is numerical *identity* Collingwood means when he speaks of "re-enactment." If Collingwood's act were a *re-enactment* of Euclid's, his act would be *numerically identical* with Euclid's rather than merely *exactly similar* to it. Collingwood's opponent asserts that these two acts are exactly similar but numerically different—they are two different acts. And so he denies that Collingwood's act is a re-enactment of Euclid's act.

Why does Collingwood's opponent hold this view? Collingwood describes the opponent's reasons for holding this view as follows:

It is contended by our supposed objector that Euclid's act of thought and mine are not one but two: numerically two though specifically one. It is also contended that my act of now thinking "the angles are equal" stands in the same relation to my act of thinking "the angles are equal" five minutes ago. The reason why this seems quite certain to the objector is, I believe, that he conceives an act of thought as something that has its place in the flow of consciousness, whose being is simply its occurrence in that flow. Once it has happened, the flow carries it into the past, and nothing can recall it. Another of the same kind may happen, but not that again.[6]

The passage shows that by "re-enactment," Collingwood means "performance of that numerically identical act again." And re-enactment of the intentions of past agents is the task of the historian. This is the way in which parts of the past are brought into the present. Since Collingwood believes that historical knowledge is knowledge of past intentions, if re-enactment of past intentions is possible, then historical knowledge is possible because the historian can then have direct knowledge of the past. By showing that such re-enactments are possible Collingwood attempts to refute the sceptic.

How does Collingwood try to prove that acts of thought, including intentions, can be revived or resurrected and thus brought into the present? His argument involves two cases: *Case I*—a person thinking "the angles are equal" for five seconds; *Case II*—the person thinking "the angles are equal" for five seconds, then thinking about something else for three seconds, and then thinking "the angles are equal" again. It should be noticed that Collingwood's opponent believes that there are at least two criteria of identity and difference for acts of thought. That is, two features determine whether one act is or is not numerically identical to another act when the two are exactly similar. These features are: (a) temporal properties and (b) sameness or difference of persons. The

opponent claims that two acts are not identical if they are
located at different points in time (that is, have different
temporal properties) or are enacted by different persons.
Collingwood uses Cases I and II to examine the first of
these, that is, the contention that one criterion of difference of acts is either the mere passage of time or else
difference of location in time.

First of all, Collingwood asks how many acts of thought
the person performs in Case I:

Is he performing one act of thought sustained over those five
seconds; or is he performing five, or ten, or twenty acts of
thought numerically different but specifically identical? If the
latter, how many go to five seconds? The objector is bound to
answer this question, for the essence of his view is that acts of
thought are numerically distinct and therefore numerable. Nor
can he defer answering until he has appealed to further research,
for example in the psychological laboratory: if he does not already know what constitutes the plurality of acts of thought, the
psychology laboratory can never tell him. But any answer he
gives must be both arbitrary and self-contradictory. There is no
more reason to correlate the unity of a single act of thought
with the time lapse of one second, or a quarter of a second, than
with any other. The only possible answer is that the act of
thought is one act sustained through five seconds. . . .[7]

Collingwood is claiming that there is only one act of
thought being performed by the person in Case I. Any
reason the opponent might give for saying that there was a
certain number (greater than one) of acts performed during those five seconds would also be a reason for saying
that there was any other number—even an infinite number
—of acts performed in that interval of five seconds. Since
any other answer the opponent might give would be arbitrary in this way, the opponent must say that there is only
one act performed in that interval. Therefore, Collingwood
concludes, mere passage of time is not a criterion of difference for acts of thought.

But of course the opponent would never claim that mere
passage of time is such a criterion. He would be perfectly
happy to say that there was only one act of thought in

Case I, because he could point out that Case I differs from the Euclid–Collingwood case in which he (the opponent) said that there were two acts of thought. The difference between the Euclid–Collingwood case and Case I is that in the latter the act of thought is temporally continuous while in the former there is a temporal interval (of approximately two thousand years) between Euclid's act and Collingwood's act. In the Euclid–Collingwood case there is not only *passage of time* but also *temporal discontinuity*. And the opponent would claim that temporal discontinuity is a criterion of numerical difference of acts of thought. Thus the opponent would urge, Case I (which deals only with mere passage of time) does not refute his position.

This may be why Collingwood next uses Case II. Of Case II he says:

Have we here two acts of thought and not one, because a time elapsed between them? Clearly not; there is one single act, this time not merely sustained, but revived after an interval. For there is no difference in this case that was not already present in the other [Case I]. When an act is sustained over five seconds, the activity in the fifth second is just as much separated by a lapse of time from that in the first, as when the intervening seconds are occupied by an activity of a different kind or (if that is possible) by none.[8]

If Collingwood is using Case II to show that *temporal discontinuity* is not a criterion of difference of acts of thought, he has not succeeded in doing so. In the passage just quoted, Collingwood says that the activities of the first and fifth seconds are separated by a lapse of time in both Cases I and II; and he seems to claim that this proves the following: if the opponent says that only one act of thought is performed in Case I, then he must also say that only one act of thought is performed in Case II. That is, Collingwood seems to think that Cases I and II are exactly similar in all relevant respects, and therefore that Case II must be regarded as exhibiting revival, resurrection, or re-enactment of the numerically same act because there is only one act in Case I. When the person in Case II thinks "the angles are equal" again, he is reviving, resurrecting, or re-enacting the identical act that he performed during the first five seconds of Case II. This must be so, Collingwood claims, because the opponent has to say that only one act was performed in Case II since he says that only one act was performed in Case I.

But this does not answer the opponent. The opponent can agree that mere lapse of time is not a criterion of difference; and in that respect Cases I and II are the same, as Collingwood claims. But the opponent is claiming that *temporal discontinuity* is a criterion of difference. Case II does contain a temporal discontinuity, whereas Case I does not. And the opponent would assert that *for this reason* Case II contains two acts of thought, whereas Case I contains only one. Collingwood does seem to say that Cases I and II are exactly similar in all relevant respects. He therefore must believe that temporal discontinuity is not relevant to sameness and difference of acts of thought. But he has not proved that it is not relevant and therefore has not refuted his opponent at this point. In fact there is reason to believe that temporal discontinuity is relevant to numerical sameness and difference of entities. After all, spatial discontinuity is relevant to numerical sameness and difference of physical objects: two physical objects are numerically two and not one partly because there is or can be empty space between them. So Collingwood must prove that temporal discontinuity is not relevant to numerical sameness and difference of acts of thought in order to refute his opponent at this point. He has to prove in this way that a past act can be brought into the present in order to prove that historians can know parts of the past directly. If they can know parts of the past directly, then they do not need evidence in order to know about the past. And therefore the sceptic's argument (given in the first section) purporting to show that there could not be evidence about the past would not show that there could not be historical knowledge.

But perhaps we can give an argument to show that

temporal discontinuity need not indicate difference of acts of thought (even though Collingwood does not give such an argument). Consider the following case: a physical object X disappears suddenly and two seconds later an object exactly similar to X appears in exactly the same location where X had been. We can say either one of two things here: (i) we can say that object X has reappeared in its previous location; (ii) we can say that a different object exactly similar to X has appeared in X's previous location. Which of these would we say? It seems that we could say that either (i) or (ii) is the case. Which of these that we do say here seems to be entirely up to us. The criteria of numerical identity of physical objects do not cover cases of this sort. But this case involving X is very much like Case II involving acts of thought. And if we can say either (i) or (ii) in the case involving X, why can't we say either (i) or (ii) in Case II? If we did say (i) in Case II, then we would be saying that the numerically same act of thought reappeared after three seconds. This would be to *stipulate* that these acts are numerically identical. This stipulation would allow an act to be both past and present. And that this stipulation can be made may give some support to Collingwood's contention that parts of the past can be known.

Collingwood's opponent says that temporal discontinuity is relevant to numerical sameness and difference. His argument might be that since spatial discontinuity is relevant to numerical difference of physical objects, it is plausible to assert that temporal discontinuity is relevant to numerical difference of acts of thought because the case of physical objects tends to show that discontinuity *in itself* may be relevant to numerical difference. But, as shown above, Collingwood may reply (though he does not do so) that if we consider *temporal* discontinuity with respect to a *physical* object (as in the above case of object X), we find that temporal discontinuity does not necessarily indicate numerical difference of physical objects. And this tends to show that *temporal* discontinuity does not necessarily indicate numerical difference of acts of thought. So Collingwood can say that the numerically same act of thought is revived in Case II even though there is temporal discontinuity in Case II.

We noted earlier that the opponent claims that two things indicate numerical difference of acts: (a) temporal properties and (b) difference of persons. If the argument just given for Collingwood's position is sound, then temporal properties (lapse of time and temporal discontinuity) cannot serve as a criterion of numerical difference of acts. Let us next consider difference of persons in relation to numerical difference of acts. The opponent claims that if two acts are enacted by different persons, as in the Euclid–Collingwood case, those acts are numerically different acts. This claim is one with which Collingwood must deal because the historian and the past agent whose thoughts the historian is re-enacting are typically not the same person.

Collingwood dismisses difference of persons in one sentence: "Granted that the same act can happen twice in different contexts within the complex of my own activities, why should it not happen twice in two different complexes?"[9] The opponent would reply: The difference between complexes (that is, between persons) is a much greater difference than the difference between contexts within the same complex; therefore one cannot infer from a fact about one complex, namely, that the same act can be revived within it, to the same fact about two different complexes, namely, that the same act can be present within each of them.

But perhaps we can provide a better argument for Collingwood's position that difference in persons does not necessarily indicate a numerical difference in acts. It does seem plausible to say that there are different acts when different people perform them. But we are not forced to say this. For we can also say that difference of persons merely gives us two *ways of referring* to the numerically same thing, in the same way in which the relation of the planet Venus to both the morning and the evening gives us two ways of referring to that planet, namely as the Morning Star and as the Evening Star. Since the same act is related to two different people, we can refer to that numerically same act as Euclid's act of thought and as Collingwood's act of thought. That these are different ways of referring does not prove that different acts are being referred to by the use of these expressions.

Is Collingwood's Position Satisfactory?

Collingwood claims that the historian's act of thought can be identical in every respect with the past agent's act of thought. This is his reason for saying that parts of the past can be brought into the present and thus known directly (as opposed to being known indirectly through the use of evidence). What does he mean when he says that the past agent's act of thought and the historian's act of thought are *completely* identical? Surely there is *some* difference between the two acts, namely they are performed at different times. Yet Collingwood seems to want to allow no difference at all between these two acts. This situation may be analogized to that of perception. If one person perceives the same physical object at different times, the "*perceivings*" are at least numerically different, because "numerical difference" in this case partly means "difference in temporal location." "Perceivings," or acts of perception, are acts; and if acts of perception can differ numerically owing to temporal differences, then acts of thought may also differ numerically for the same reason because both types of acts are species of the same genus, namely *acts*.

Furthermore, Collingwood denies that his act of thought is numerically different from Euclid's even though the two acts differ in temporal location. So he does believe that it is *possible* for two acts of thought to differ numerically; he merely denies that the two acts in the Euclid–Collingwood case *do* differ numerically. But when *would* two acts of thought differ numerically for Collingwood if they do not do so when they have different temporal locations? Presumably the act of thinking "the angles are equal" and the act of thinking "the sides are equal" are numerically different. But they are also specifically different. So can numerical difference occur only when specific difference also occurs? It seems that Collingwood would say this is the case. And he probably would try to defend this thesis that numerical difference between acts exists *only* in cases of specific difference by saying that there cannot be any such thing as mere numerical difference between acts. Some *other* difference must also be present in order for two things to differ numerically. But some other difference *is* present in the Euclid–Collingwood case, namely, a difference in temporal location. So Collingwood's opponent is not asserting that there is such a thing as mere numerical difference. The opponent agrees that some other difference must also be present in order for numerical difference also to be present. Thus, why does Collingwood restrict the term "numerical difference" to cases of acts in which there is also specific difference in other respects than spatial and temporal respects? This restriction seems to be arbitrary on his part. And restricting the use of this term in this way does not eliminate the difference in temporal locations of the two acts in the Euclid–Collingwood case. So, clearly, Collingwood must admit that there is *some* difference between these two acts, namely, a difference in temporal location, whether or not he chooses to call this difference a "numerical" difference.

Clearly, if Collingwood's view is to be at all plausible, it must allow such differences in temporal location. Alan Donagan claims that Collingwood distinguishes between act and enactment:

If both act and re-enactment are brought under the concept of the doing of an act (or its "enactment"), they are obviously different enactments. Collingwood made this plain in his terminology, when he described historians as *re*-enacting, *re*-thinking, or *re*viving past thoughts. Considered as enactments, an enactment and its re-enactment are not the same.[10]

Donagan's evidence that Collingwood made this distinction seems to be Collingwood's use of such terms as "re-enactment." Let us assume that Collingwood did make this distinction. If he did so, it is very probable that he did so in order to express differences in temporal location. *Differences in temporal location pertain to enactments, not to acts.* (In fact, as pointed out later, he claims that *acts* do not have temporal location at all. *Only* enactments have temporal location.) Thus, different enactments have different temporal locations even though the numerically same act can be enacted in these different enactments. Difference in temporal location produces difference in enactments, but not in acts. So Collingwood would say that the numerically same act can be enacted at different times.

One might object here that if Collingwood makes this distinction between act and enactment, he weakens his answer to the sceptic. For the existence of different enactments allows the possibility that *what* is enacted each time is different, and hence allows the possibility that the historian does not re-enact the past agent's intention. But the following reply can be made to this objection: Collingwood is not trying to guarantee that, in each case, the historian does succeed in re-enacting the past agent's intention; rather, he is only trying to demonstrate the *possibility* of the historian's performing such a re-enactment and thus demonstrate the possibility of historical knowledge. It is this *possibility*—the possibility of a part of the past also being present or the possibility of now enacting the numerically same thing that was previously enacted—that the sceptic denies.

But there are several important objections which can be raised regarding Collingwood's position:

(1) If two enactments of one act are to be *two* enact-

ments, then they *must* differ in temporal location. Collingwood seems to be using the term "enactment" in such a way that *two* enactments *must* be numerically different from one another in the way in which, according to Collingwood, exactly similar *acts* of thought *cannot* be numerically different (since he believes that *acts* are numerically different only if they are specifically different, that is, not exactly similar). But if difference in temporal location does not make a numerical difference in acts, why does it make a numerical difference in enactments? Couldn't the same arguments which Collingwood gives for the lack of such difference in acts be given for the lack of such difference in enactments? For instance, does an *enactment* occur over a period of time? How many *enactments* are there in a five minute period of thinking "the angles are equal"? Couldn't arguments very similar to those which Collingwood gives with respect to acts be used to show that there is only one enactment in Case II? If so, then temporal discontinuity does not make a numerical difference in *enactments* either.

(2) Furthermore, an act *is* (partly) an enactment. It seems odd to speak of an *act* being enacted. An act would seem to be "composed" of its content and an enactment. An enactment is part of an act rather than something which happens to an act. If so, then the existence of different enactments entails the existence of different acts. There cannot be one act which is enacted several times, if an enactment is part of an act. For if the act is enacted several times, then the act performed the second time has a different component (namely, its enactment) from the act performed the first time. And if these two components of these acts are different, the acts themselves are different. So the same act is not enacted, and hence is not re-enacted, contrary to what Collingwood says, at different times.

(3) Another sort of problem about the relation between acts and enactments arises in the following way. The enactment of an act and the *re*-enactment of that same act

must differ in temporal location, since an enactment which occurs simultaneously with another cannot be a *re*-enactment of what was enacted in the other. And one can always ask *when* a certain enactment took place. (In fact, as we have seen, temporal location seems to be an essential property of enactments.) But, according to Collingwood, acts have no relation to time at all. "It is not only the object of thought that somehow stands outside time; the act of thought does so too. . . ."[11] But if an act is essentially related to its various enactments—an act, after all, cannot exist apart from some enactment of it—and if enactments are essentially related to time, then the act is somehow related to time. Collingwood's position is unacceptable until it is made clear how an act can be intimately related to an essentially temporal entity (its enactment) and still "stand outside" time.

Collingwood and Historical Scepticism

It is often alleged that Collingwood was influenced by Croce with respect to the philosophy of history. Even if this is true for other aspects of Collingwood's theory of history, two important aspects of his theory show none of Croce's influence. The first is Collingwood's belief that the aim of the historian is to know about the past. Croce regarded the historian's task as constructing an acceptable interpretation of the documents, not as discovering facts about the past. Since Collingwood believes the historian does have this latter task, he attempts to refute scepticism about the possibility of historical knowledge, whereas Croce regards certain arguments of the sceptic as sound. This brings us to the second important difference between Croce and Collingwood. Croce believes that the historian must construct human thought and feeling, as does Collingwood.[12] But Collingwood claims, as Croce did not, that this consists in *re*-enactments of acts of thought, in order to refute scepticism.

The sceptic claims that there cannot be evidence about

the past (see p. 64). Collingwood tries to refute the
sceptic by first asserting that historical knowledge consists
in knowledge of past intentions (pp. 65–69) and then trying to prove that past intentions can be brought into the
present (pp. 69–74). If past intentions can be brought into
the present, they can be *directly* known by the historian. If
we can have *direct* knowledge of the past—knowledge of
the past by, so to speak, directly inspecting the past after it
has been brought into the present—then even if the sceptic
is correct in saying that there cannot be evidence about the
past, he has not succeeded in showing that historical
knowledge is impossible. For if such evidence cannot be
had, this shows only that *indirect* knowledge of the past
cannot be had. But if Collingwood is right, we can nevertheless have *direct* knowledge of the past; and therefore we
can have knowledge of the past, thus showing the sceptic's
conclusion to be false. I have tried to show (pp. 74–81)
that certain arguments can be given for Collingwood's
position, but that, nevertheless, he does not succeed in
proving that position to be correct. The sceptic can reply
that Collingwood gives no criterion for determining when
a *re*-enactment, as distinguished from an enactment that
only appears to be a *re*-enactment, has taken place. But
even if such a criterion can be provided, there are serious
objections, as shown above, to the notions of act and
enactment as used by Collingwood. Hence Collingwood
has not succeeded in refuting the sceptic.

I have discussed only that part of Collingwood's theory
of history that has to do with acts and re-enactments because this is the core of his attempt to refute scepticism
(and of his own theory of history). I have tried to show
that he does not succeed in refuting the sceptic. If he had
succeeded in this, it would be acceptable to regard historians as discovering facts about the past because they could
bring parts of the past into the present. But since he has
not succeeded, the theory that history consists or should
consist in creation and construction rather than in discovery and interpretation may still be maintained.

PART

III

The form of, or argument for, scepticism about the possibility of knowledge of the past that has received most discussion in recent philosophy of history is called "Historical Relativism." If Relativism were sound, then it would provide a basis for scepticism and hence provide a basis for a Construction Theory of History. I believe that Relativism is not sound. I also believe that, although it is not sound, many of the putative refutations of it that have been given do not show that it is not sound. Accordingly, in Chapter Four I will discuss some examples of certain types of refutations that have been offered, my purpose being to show that none of them succeeds in refuting Relativism. In Chapter Five I shall first distinguish between two types of Relativism, which I call "First-Level" and "Second-Level." Then I offer a refutation of both types of Relativism.

If I am correct in believing that Relativism is unsound, then scepticism about historical knowledge of the past must be based on different arguments. Some of these more satisfactory arguments will be given in Part IV.

CHAPTER FOUR

𗀱𗀱𗀱𗀱𗀱𗀱𗀱𗀱𗀱

HISTORICAL RELATIVISM I

Introduction

Historical relativism is a type of scepticism about the possibility of historical knowledge. It holds that all historical judgments are and must be relative, subjective or biased; and because all such judgments are biased, none of them are true. None of them accurately represents past events. They represent partly the way in which some historian regards those past events. Since historians use various standards and values in dealing with evidence, the bias inherent in those standards and values must inevitably influence the use made of that evidence and the interpretation of the past based on that evidence; thus, inevitably, his bias will distort and in this way render false the historian's account of the past. Therefore there can be no historical knowledge. We will call this thesis that all historical judgments are and must be biased "the Relativist's claim."

In this chapter I will discuss several putative refutations of the Relativist's claim which are independent of any particular theory of history. Putative refutations of the Relativist's claim fall into two categories: (1) "Categorical refutations," those that deal with all forms of historical relativism at once by presenting one argument that is alleged to refute all its forms; (2) "Particular refutations," those dealing with each form of relativism individually by presenting different replies to different arguments for the Relativist's claim. The three putative refutations to be discussed in this chapter are all intended to be categorical refutations.

What is meant by saying that standards and values influence the historian's account of the past and render it biased? There are two ways in which this influence can manifest itself: (1) they influence what the historian takes to be reliable evidence; (2) they influence what interpretation he builds on the evidence in two respects: (a) they influence the type of explanations he gives of the occurrence of past events; (b) they influence the evaluations he makes of those events. An example of (1) might be as follows: Suppose the historian is of a certain political persuasion; he comes across a diary written, it appears, by someone of the opposite political persuasion; the historian should allow for the diarist's bias resulting from his political views; but if the historian does more than this, for example, if he completely discounts the value of the diary as a picture of the life of the diarist's times because he believes people of the diarist's political persuasion are unreliable observers, the historian's own values and, in particular, his standards of what counts as reliable evidence are influencing his account of those times in such a way as to render that account biased.

An instance of values and standards influencing what historians take to be reliable evidence is described by J. C. Holt in his pamphlet on King John.[1] Nineteenth-century historians such as Stubbs had two types of evidence pertaining to King John and his reign: contemporary chronicles and narratives on the one hand and records (such as Chancery and household enrollments) on the other. The nineteenth-century historians relied on the contemporary accounts. But modern historians rely mainly on the records. In fact, Holt states that " . . . the record evidence is now the main force and the narrative simply reinforcement; where the two conflict the contemporary narrative is normally rejected; chronicle evidence unsupported by record is viewed with suspicion."[2] The Relativist would attribute this change in what type of evidence is taken to be reliable to a difference in the standards and values of nineteenth- and twentieth-century historians.

Croce gives possible examples of the second sort of influence standards and values can have when he cites as examples of "poetical history" "Droysen giving expression to his lyrical aspiration toward the strong centralized state in his history of Macedonia, that Prussia of Hellas; Grote to his aspirations toward democratic institutions, as symbolized in Athens; Mommsen to those directed toward empire, as symbolized in Caesar. . . ."[3] Because Grote valued democratic institutions very highly, he perhaps emphasized the democratic aspects of Athenian society without giving due weight to the undemocratic aspects. Because Droysen valued the centralized state highly, he perhaps overemphasized the positive effects of Macedonia in the Hellenistic period, while underemphasizing its negative or undesirable effects. Thus, their accounts may be biased.

Bias stems from other sorts of standards and values also. For example, a Catholic historian may consider the Reformation as a setback in the onward progress of Christianity, whereas a Protestant historian might regard it as a return to true Christianity. A Marxist will give one interpretation to the Russian Revolution; a social democrat will give another. Not only will they evaluate the desirability of the Revolution differently, but also they will emphasize different factors as causes in explaining the occurrence of the Revolution. The Marxist will cite exclusively economic causes, whereas the social democrat may give much weight to the personalities of Lenin, Trotsky, and others.

None of these biased accounts can represent the truth about the past, according to the Relativist. Each of these accounts emphasizes certain factors while de-emphasizing others in explaining and evaluating events. All of these factors were present in the case of each event, according to the Relativist, and what is needed is to give each of them its proper weight in order to give a true picture of the past. But every historian has some bias or other. Hence none can give each factor its proper weight. To do so would require a historian with no bias whatsoever. The Relativist would deny that it is possible to have a historian with no bias whatsoever, since, for one reason, every historian uses evidence and *must* have some standards to use in evaluating that evidence. The Relativist seems to claim that the use of any standards and values inevitably results in a biased account. Hence, he would conclude, it is not possible for any historian to give a true picture of the past, since all historians *must* use some standards and values. But why couldn't there be a set of standards and values the use of which *does* give due weight to every factor? The Relativist would say that, by definition of "standards and values," giving due weight to each factor can result only from not using any standards and values. But a historian is one who attempts to gain knowledge of the past through the use of evidence. And evidence can be evaluated only by the use of some set of standards and values. (We will see, in connection with Second-Level Relativism, that a Relativist could admit that there is a correct set of standards and values and that some historical judgments are true, and yet still maintain that a certain version of relativism was nevertheless correct and that there could be no historical knowledge.)

The relation between standards and values on the one hand and the historian's particular judgments on the other is not one of entailment. That is, certain particular judgments are not entailed by certain standards and values together with certain "brute facts" as evidence. The relation between these is weaker than entailment. By saying that standards and values "influence" particular judgments, I mean that given a certain set of standards and values and a certain group of "brute facts," certain particular judgments will seem reasonable or plausible to the historian in question and others will seem less plausible or wholly implausible to him.

In the next sections of this chapter I will try to show that three examples of commonly given objections to Relativism in fact do not succeed in refuting that position.

Nagel: Bias Can Be Identified and Corrected

Ernest Nagel has given two putative refutations of historical relativism, the first of which goes as follows: (1) the assertion that historical judgments are biased assumes that there is a distinction between biased and unbiased judgments; (2) it follows from this, according to Nagel, that the bias can be identified; (3) it follows from (2) that it is possible that the bias can be corrected.[4] This is a putative categorical refutation because it is intended to refute any type of position which holds that historical judgments are biased, regardless of the reasons given for that position.

In saying in (2) that the bias can be identified, Nagel probably means that biased judgments can be identified, that is, that one can determine which judgments are biased and which are not. If, instead, he means that one can determine in what way a biased judgment is biased, then it is not clear that (2) follows from (1), for one could know what it means for a judgment to be biased without being able to tell in what way a particular judgment is biased. So we will interpret (2) in the first way rather than the second.

Is Nagel's argument sound when (2) is interpreted in the first way? The Relativist would have to admit that (1) is true. He would also admit that (2) is true, even if (2) does not follow from (1); for the Relativist claims to know both *that* there is bias in historical judgments and *which* historical judgments are biased, since, after all, he claims that *all* historical judgments are biased. So (2) is true. And if (3) follows from (2), then the Relativist must admit that (3) is also true. But does (3) follow from (2)?

In order to show that (3) does not follow from (2), the Relativist must show that the truth of (2) is compatible with the falsity of (3). How can he show this? The Relativist might say that the fact that men in different eras form different judgments about the same past events shows

that historical judgments are biased. He would choose
cases of past events about which the same or almost the
same evidence existed in two different eras and yet people
in those different eras made different judgments about
those past events. This would show, according to the Relativist, that historical judgments are based on values and
hence are biased. For, he would claim, the only way of
accounting for different judgments in different eras on the
basis of the *same* evidence is by saying that such judgments are based on values and that different values were
prevalent in those different eras. Thus, the Relativist would
admit that (2) is true; *all* historical judgments, being
based on values, are biased. But it does not follow from
this that such bias can be corrected. Historians *must* use
evidence, and hence they *must* evaluate that evidence.
They evaluate that evidence as reliable, significant, and so
on, on the basis of certain values and standards. Hence it
would seem that all historical judgments, being based on
evidence, would *inevitably* be biased. Hence it does not
follow from (2) that bias can be eliminated from historical judgments. Nagel has not succeeded in refuting the
Relativist in this way.

Nagel: Is the Relativist's Claim Itself Biased?

Nagel has also attempted to refute relativism in
another way. He asks: Is the Relativist's claim itself free
from bias? If it is free from bias, then not all judgments
are biased and hence the possibility exists that not all
historical judgments are biased. If this claim is itself
biased, then ". . . its validity is narrowly self-limited, no
student with a different social perspective can properly
understand or evaluate it, and it must be dismissed as
irrelevant by most inquirers into social questions."[5] This
type of argument against relativism has also been given by
many others.

Might the Relativist reply to the first part of Nagel's
objection by saying: My claim concerns only *historical*

judgments and, since my claim itself is *not* a historical judgment, showing that my claim is unbiased will not show that *historical* judgments are possibly not biased; whether or not nonhistorical judgments (such as my claim) are free of bias proves nothing about the bias (or lack thereof) of historical judgments because nonhistorical and historical judgments are very different types of judgments; hence my claim can be unbiased without this showing that *historical* judgments can be unbiased. I believe that the Relativist cannot reply to Nagel in this way. He cannot reply in this way because (1) the Relativist's claim *is*, in a sense, a historical judgment since that claim concerns *all* historical judgments (labelling them as "subjective" or "biased"), including past historical judgments; since it is partly about *past* historical judgments, it is partly about the past and hence is itself partly a historical judgment; (2) the Relativist's claim is based on an argument from history, namely that historians in different *past* eras have judged the same events differently; hence the Relativist's claim is likely to be infected with the bias inherent (according to the Relativist himself) in the historical judgments involved in that argument from history on which his own claim is based.

The Relativist can, however, reply to Nagel in the following way. He can admit that his claim is biased and then point out that his claim is not *necessarily* invalid for others. It is certainly possible that, given *any* particular set of values, there might be some person who holds those values and yet would assert the Relativist's claim. It is the possibility of there being such a person for each set of values that is important here. It is not necessarily the case that the Relativist's claim can itself be made only on the basis of one or a limited number of sets of values. What Nagel would have to show is that there is a significant number of sets of values with which the Relativist's claim is *incompatible*. He would have to show that there is a significant number of sets of values such that a person who holds any of those sets of values could not be a

Relativist. Only then could Nagel justifiably conclude that the Relativist's claim is irrelevant to the pursuits of most social inquirers. If the claim is compatible with many or most sets of values—if, given a particular set of values, there *is* someone *or could be* someone who holds those values and yet would assert the Relativist's claim—then relativism will still pose a serious problem for such inquirers. It is not the case that a person with a certain set of values would regard the Relativist's claim as irrelevant just because he holds a different set of values from that of the Relativist, for the Relativist's claim might be capable of being asserted by someone who holds *that* person's set of values *too*. Thus Nagel has not succeeded in refuting the Relativist.

Berlin: "Subjective" and "Objective" are Correlative Terms

Another categorical refutation has been offered by Isaiah Berlin:

> Every judgment is relative, every evaluation subjective. . . . But relative to what? Subjective in contrast with what? . . . Relative terms (especially pejoratives) need correlatives, or else they turn out to be without meaning themselves. . . . Some of our judgments are, no doubt, relative and subjective, but others are not; for if none were so, if objectivity were in principle inconceivable, the terms subjective and objective, no longer contrasted, would mean nothing; for all correlatives stand and fall together.[6]

Berlin seems to be attributing three distinct positions to the Relativist: (a) there are in fact no objective historical judgments; (b) there can be no objective historical judgments; (c) objectivity in historical judgments is inconceivable. His argument is: (1) the Relativist must admit that the term "subjective" is meaningful; (2) if "subjective" is meaningful, then the term "objective" must also be meaningful; (3) if "objective" is meaningful, then objective historical judgments must be at least possible; (4) by (1) and (2), the term "objective" is meaningful; (5) by

(3) and (4), objective historical judgments are at least possible. But Berlin does not give an argument to show that the crucial premise, (3), is in fact true. Therefore, let us see if we can provide an argument for the claim that (3) is true. And let us do this by first considering the following reply by the Relativist to the argument that Berlin does give.

The Relativist might reply that his claim requires only that objectivity be conceivable in the sense that the term "objective" is meaningful. He might say that in addition to the term "objective" being meaningful, it is not also necessary that objective historical judgments be possible. That is, the Relativist would claim that (3) is false because its antecedent can be true while its consequent is false. The Relativist then might try to show that the term "objective" is meaningful by giving the following definition of the expression "objective historical judgment": an objective historical judgment is one that is true, that is, in some way corresponds to or agrees with that part of the past with which it deals. By giving the term "objective" a use in connection with the expression "historical judgment," the Relativist gives a meaning to the term "objective". In defense of this definition, the Relativist might say that (a) all true judgments are objective, since subjectivity (that is, nonobjectivity) is a sufficient condition of falsity; and (b) all objective judgments are true, that is, that subjectivity is also a necessary condition of falsity, because all falsity is due to misuse of the evidence in one way or another, for example, by not giving enough weight to certain pieces of evidence due to the holding of certain values. Of course, one might deny (b) on the grounds that subjectivity is not the only cause of falsity—lack of sufficient evidence also can lead to falsity. But the Relativist might answer by saying that it is the values that the historian holds which lead him to regard insufficient evidence as sufficient and thus this too is a type of misuse of the evidence. The definition of the expression "subjective historical judgment" would then be: A subjective historical judgment is one that is false; such judgments are false for a certain reason, namely, because they are based on certain values and standards relative to the historian's own era.

The Relativist is denying that (3) is true; he is denying the claim that if the term "objective" is meaningful, objective historical judgments must be at least possible. He is trying to show that the term "objective" can be meaningful without objective historical judgments' being possible. That is, he is trying to prove that the antecedent of (3) can be true while the consequent of (3) is false, and thus that (3) itself is false. He has given a definition in order to show that the term "objective" is meaningful, thus showing the antecedent of (3) to be true. But he still has to show that given this definition, objective historical judgments are not possible, in order to show that the consequent of (3) is false. The impossibility of objective historical judgments does not follow from this definition alone; the Relativist must give an additional argument to show that objective historical judgments are not possible even though the term "objective" is meaningful.

One such additional argument, which has already been given (see pp. 89–90) and which I will call "Argument R," would be as follows: "There can be no objective historical judgments because all historical judgments are *necessarily* made on the basis of standards and values; historical judgments are, by definition, judgments about the past made on the basis of evidence; a historian is a person who makes such judgments *on the basis of evidence*; someone who knows about the past directly without using evidence or by means of some form of intuition would not be a historian; but any judgment about the past made on the basis of evidence, that is, any historical judgment, must involve the application of standards and values because the evidence must be evaluated in order to be usable; and because such judgments necessarily involve standards and values in this way (as the King John case described earlier shows), they necessarily are subjective; that is, there cannot be a historical judgment that is not subjective; that is, objective historical judgments are impossible."

Argument R is intended to show that historical judgments *must* be subjective and hence (by the Relativist's definition of "subjective") cannot be true. But it is clear that the Relativist cannot give Argument R, for if he does, it follows that every assertion that a particular judgment is an objective historical judgment not only is false but also entails a contradiction. For example, let us take the assertion "Judgment X is an objective historical judgment." It follows from this assertion together with the Relativist's definition of "objective historical judgment" that Judgment X is true. But it also follows from this assertion together with Argument R that Judgment X is not true, since Judgment X is a historical judgment. So if this assertion is true and if the Relativist is correct, it is also true that Judgment X is both true and not true. Thus, this assertion, together with the definition of "objective historical judgment" and Argument R, entails a contradiction. In the same way, the assertion "This geometrical figure is a square circle," together with the definitions of "square" and "circle," entails a contradiction, for example, "this geometrical figure has a center (because it is a circle) and does not have a center (because it is a square)." That this assertion entails a contradiction shows that the expression "square circle" is without meaning. Similarly, that the assertion "Judgment X is an objective historical judgment" entails a contradiction shows that the expression "objective historical judgment" is without meaning. So if the Relativist does give Argument R, he cannot give the definition of the expression "objective historical judgment" he does give, for that definition does not give that expression any meaning. And since he has not given the expression "objective historical judgment" any meaning, he has not succeeded in giving the term "objective" a meaning.

Hence if the Relativist does give Argument R, he may succeed in showing that objective historical judgments are impossible, but he has not *also* shown that the expression "objective historical judgment" and the term "objective" are meaningful. Hence he has not shown that the antecedent of (3) is true, even though he may have shown that the consequent of (3) is false. Therefore he has not shown (3) to be false.

This gives some support to Berlin's contention that (3) is true. It tends to show that an argument (such as Argument R) which proves the impossibility of objective historical judgments will also prove that the expression "objective historical judgment" is meaningless. It thus tends to show that if the Relativist does say that the term "objective" is meaningful, he must say that objective historical judgments are at least possible. And if Berlin is correct about correlatives, the Relativist must say that the term "objective" is meaningful because he believes that the term "subjective" is meaningful.

But does showing the possibility of such judgments amount to showing the untenability of historical relativism? Of course, that objective historical judgments are possible does not imply that any such judgments in fact exist. But that they are at least possible seems to render the Relativist's challenge to historians far less serious than it might at first be taken to be. Berlin's categorical refutation, when expanded in the way indicated above, seems to show that historical judgments are at least not *incorrigibly* subjective, contrary to what Relativists usually claim.

Is Berlin's Attempted Refutation of Relativism Satisfactory?

Nevertheless, Berlin's attempted categorical refutation is not cogent for at least three reasons.

(1) Berlin claims that "subjective" and "objective" are correlatives, but he does not tell how to determine that two terms are correlatives. According to Berlin, correlatives are terms each of which must be meaningful in order for the other term to be meaningful. Since this is what Berlin

wants to assert about correlatives, he must give us some *other* way of determining whether or not two terms are correlatives. The Relativist might admit that *if* "subjective" and "objective" are correlatives, then one must be meaningful if the other is to be meaningful, and at the same time he might deny that they are in fact correlatives. Berlin does not give us some general criterion for determining whether or not two terms are correlatives.

Perhaps Berlin regards his remarks about correlatives as following from a general theory of meaning. For example, he may believe that every term in the language has a correlative term. But this is not true. What, for example, would be the correlative of the noun "clock"? Of course, Berlin might say that this theory of meaning applies only to adjectives (like "subjective" and "objective"), not to nouns. But given any adjective, we can form its noun cognate and it seems reasonable to expect that this theory would hold good for those noun cognates (for instance, "subjectivism" and "objectivism") if it holds good for the adjectives. Furthermore, we still need a criterion for determining *which* of the other terms in the language is the correlative of the term in question.

(2) Suppose the terms "subjective" and "objective" have somehow been shown to be correlatives. The argument given above for the truth of Berlin's proposition (3) is cogent only because the Relativist gave a certain reason for regarding historical judgments as irremediably subjective, along with a certain definition intended to show that, in spite of this, the term "objective" is meaningful. But perhaps the Relativist can give another definition that shows the term "objective" to be meaningful and yet which does not conflict, in the way indicated earlier (pp. 95–96), with the argument for the subjectivity of all historical judgments.

The Relativist might provide such a definition in the following way. Historical judgments are assertions about the past which are made on the basis of evidence. But not all assertions about the past are or need necessarily be based on evidence, as historical judgments must be based. For example, the assertions of an omniscient Being, such as God, about the past would not be based on evidence, for such a Being would not need to use evidence. Such a Being would know the past directly and hence would not make *historical* judgments about the past. So the Relativist could give a meaning or a use to the term "objective" by defining the expression "objective assertion about the past" rather than by defining the expression "objective historical judgment." He would define "objective assertion about the past" as "a true assertion about the past," and would maintain that since *historical* judgments are based on evidence, by Argument R they cannot be objective assertions about the past. But there *can* be objective assertions about the past, for example, those made by an omniscient Being. This would therefore provide a meaning or a use for "objective" in connection with a class of assertions (namely, assertions about the past) of which historical judgments form a subclass, and yet rule out the possibility of there being objective historical judgments. Hence the antecedent of (3) is true because the term "objective" is meaningful; for now there can be assertions about the past, for example, those made by an omniscient Being, which can be stated to be objective without the statement that *they* are objective being such as to entail a contradiction; for *they* are not historical judgments; but the consequent of (3) is false because, by the Relativist's Argument R, there cannot be any objective *historical* judgments. And since its antecedent is true and its consequent is false, (3) is itself false. Hence Berlin's attempted refutation of relativism is not sound.

(3) Even if the preceding two objections to Berlin's position can be answered, there remains a third very important objection. The Relativist could admit the possibility of true historical judgments, as Berlin claims that he must; he could even admit the *existence* of true historical judgments. But he could say that although some of the

judgments made by historians *are* true and are objective, we cannot tell *which* these are. We have no way of distinguishing true historical judgments from false ones. So far this position is that of scepticism about historical knowledge; but it is not yet that form of scepticism known as "Relativism." It becomes a type of Relativism when the following reason is given for this sceptical position: All judgments are based on standards and values; only those judgments based on the correct standards and values will possibly be true; but we have no standards and values on the basis of which we can evaluate standards and values; therefore we cannot determine which standards are correct and hence cannot determine which judgments are correct or are objective, even though some are. We will call this position "Second-Level Relativism." This form of relativism does present a serious challenge to the historian. But Second-Level Relativism is compatible with the truth of the conclusion of Berlin's argument (namely, that objective historical judgments are *possible*) because it is willing to admit (or is equally compatible with) the truth of a proposition (namely, that objective historical judgments *have been made*) which is *stronger* than Berlin's conclusion. So Berlin's conclusion and Second-Level Relativism can both be true at the same time. Hence Berlin's argument does not refute Second-Level Relativism.[7]

Is Historical Relativism Sound?

Two of the three putative categorical refutations that have been discussed are often used against Relativism. It is often maintained that Relativism is a doctrine that refutes itself because if the Relativist's claim is true, then it is itself relative and hence can "be dismissed as irrelevant by most inquirers into social questions." And it is just as often said that the Relativist must regard the word "objective" as meaningful and hence that he must hold that objective historical judgments are possible. I have tried to show that these putative refutations are unsatisfactory.

Does the fact that they are unsatisfactory show Relativism to be a sound doctrine and hence a basis for the Construction Theory of History? It does not show this, for Relativism may be unsound in other respects. I believe that Relativism is not a sound doctrine and I will try to show this in the next chapter.

CHAPTER FIVE

᠍᠍᠍᠍᠍᠍᠍᠍᠍᠍

HISTORICAL RELATIVISM

Two Types of Relativism

The three putative refutations of Relativism discussed in Chapter Four represent the ways that have most often been used to refute relativism. But none of these three refutations appear to be cogent, as we have seen. Hence in this chapter I will attempt to cast doubt on the soundness of the Relativists' position in quite a different way.

There are at least two main types of historical relativism. The first type, which I shall call "First-Level Relativism" because it is concerned with particular judgments, holds that historical judgments are and must be subjective, and for that reason alone they are and must be false. The First-Level Relativist asserts that the historian's standards and values can greatly influence what evidence he uses, how he interprets each piece of evidence, and the nature of the narrative he constructs on the basis of the evidence. That is, these standards and values *can* influence historical judgments. He may also point out that different historians construct different interpretations of the past on the basis of substantially the same evidence. This proves that standards and values *do* influence the historian's judgments; that is, this proves that those judgments are biased. And the First-Level Relativist further contends that all biased judgments are false.

The second type of Relativism is what was called at the end of Chapter Four "Second-Level Relativism." I call it "Second-Level" because it is concerned with the values that influence particular judgments. These values influence many particular judgments and in this sense are more general than, and on a higher level than, particular judgments. Second-Level Relativism admits that some particular judgments may be objective and hence true, but it holds that since historical judgments are determined at least in part by the historian's standards and values, determining *which* judgments are objective depends on first being able to determine which standards and values are correct or ought to be used. Objective judgments are those based on the correct standards and values.

It can be objected to First-Level Relativism that the First-Level Relativist gives no reason to believe that there cannot be a correct set of standards and values, that is, a set whose use results in due weight being given to each factor and each type of evidence. This objection, however, cannot be made to Second-Level Relativism because the Second-Level Relativist admits that there can be a correct set of standards and values. But, the Second-Level Relativist continues, it cannot be determined which are the correct standards and values because there are no higher or second-order standards and values by which to judge first-order standards and values. Or if there are such second-order standards and values, the problem of deciding which second-order set is the correct set to use then arises, so that a third-order set is needed in order to judge second-order sets of standards and values. And a still higher set would be required to judge the third-order sets. Thus an infinite regress develops. This infinite regress is vicious because, being infinite, it cannot be traversed and yet it must be traversed if one is to know which first-order set of standards and values to use to evaluate particular judgments as to their truth or falsity. Hence one can never determine which, if any, of these particular judgments are objective.

These two types of Relativism are distinct. The First-Level Relativist asserts that all historical judgments are false merely in virtue of being biased. Thus, according to him, one could not find that some historical judgments are true because no set of standards and values leads to true historical judgments; no such set is the "correct" set to use. The Second-Level Relativist denies that historical judgments are subjective and therefore false merely because they are influenced by standards and values. According to the Second-Level Relativist, some of these judgments may be objective and true because they are based on the correct standards and values; that is, some particular judgments may correctly represent past events. But though he admits that some historical judgments may be objective, he denies that one can determine *which* historical judgments are objective.

In the following section, I will discuss the concept of objectivity, that is, what the term "objective" means. I will try to show what at least one very important kind of objectivity consists in. After that, I will show how the possibility of this sort of objectivity proves relativism to be unsound.

The Concept of Objectivity

The Second-Level Relativist asserts that we have no standards by which to judge standards and, consequently, cannot determine which historical judgments are objective and hence true. But, of course, it can be argued that this situation prevails in all fields, including the sciences. It might at first seem that there is a standard by which to judge standards in the sciences; for example, scientific standards are "correct" if they make possible the production of certain desirable practical results. But this does not show that those standards are therefore "true"; it merely shows that they are useful. So the Second-Level Relativist's objections concerning the absence of second-level standards and values would tend to show that all disciplines involve the sort of subjectivity he attributes to history.

Yet the Second-Level Relativist typically believes that history is in a worse position in this respect than is science.

In fact, science is often taken to be the paradigm of objectivity by all varieties of relativists. So our question is: What is the difference between science and history such that science is objective and history is not?

There are analogues in science to the historian's standards and values. Let us take the so-called "principle of simplicity" as an example. This principle urges that of two hypotheses both of which account for all of the experimental facts, the simpler one is to be adopted. This principle and others provide a general guide for scientific inferences in a way similar to that in which the historian's standards and values provide a general guide for his inferences. The major, and perhaps sole, difference between science and history here is that all (or most) scientists are agreed that the principle of simplicity and others should be used, whereas historians are not agreed on any one group of standards and values.

So it seems that what is lacking in history and present in science is *agreement* rather than *truth*. Science is *objective*, whereas history is not. And scientists *agree* on standards, whereas historians do not. This strongly indicates that Relativists who insist on the objectivity of science take this sort of agreement as at least the hallmark and perhaps even the essence of objectivity. Thus, if such a Relativist claims that historical judgments are irremediably subjective—if he says that such judgments are necessarily subjective—he is claiming that there *cannot* be agreement among historians on a set of standards and values. Certainly there is at present no such agreement; furthermore, there is at present no procedure for reaching such agreement. However, the Relativist cannot infer from this that there will never be such agreement, much less that there *cannot* be such agreement.

But, more importantly, is it agreement on *standards and values* that is required in order for history to have objectivity? Perhaps we can agree with the Relativist that agreement is the hallmark of objectivity. But this does not entail that the agreement which indicates objectivity is agreement *on standards and values.* In fact, it is very likely that *that* sort of agreement is not a sign of objectivity, as will be shown below. But what sort of agreement would show history to be objective? What other kind of agreement can there be? The kind of agreement which, I believe, indicates objectivity, is agreement not on standards and values, but *on particular judgments.* For example, suppose that eventually Catholic and Protestant historians agree on an interpretation (consisting of various particular judgments) of the Reformation, while remaining Catholics and Protestants—that is, while holding to their different values. I believe that there would be a strong case for saying *this* interpretation of the Reformation is an objective interpretation, since it is something people with different values are agreed upon. I am not saying that mere agreement on particular judgments indicates objectivity. Rather, I am saying that agreement on particular judgments, *where these judgments were made on the basis of different sets of standards and values,* indicates the objectivity of those particular judgments.

One might be tempted to say of this supposed case of agreement by Catholic and Protestant historians that the interpretation about which they agree is objective not because their different standards led to the same results, but rather because these historians were able to agree *in spite of* holding different standards. That is, one might be tempted to say that the differences in their standards were irrelevant, as it turned out, to their interpretations of the Reformation. We would, presumably, always have this option of saying that historians reached agreement in spite of holding different standards rather than saying that their different standards led to the same conclusions. But to exercise this option in *every* case would be to make the Relativist's position true by stipulation. This would happen as follows: In a case of disagreement among historians, the Relativist would attribute the disagreement to their use of different standards, whereas in a case of agreement, he would say that they reached agreement in spite of holding

to different standards. Thus he would not allow that there
could be a case in which agreement was reached *on the
basis of* different standards.

If the Relativist were to maintain this position, he would
be maintaining that it is impossible for historians to agree,
as historians, on particular judgments. Historians are
people who make judgments about the past on the basis of
evidence and hence, ultimately, on the basis of standards.
If they used any other method of making judgments—for
instance, revelation—they would not be historians. But if
agreement among historians were *always* taken to be independent of the standards they use, then they would never
agree *as historians*, that is, as a result of the use of standards and values.

But can the Relativist maintain this position? Clearly,
his exercise of the option described above in every case of
agreement would merely be an *ad hoc* measure designed to
preserve his thesis about the irremediable subjectivity of
historical judgments. The Relativist cannot have it both
ways at once. If he says that disagreement among historians is *due* to their use of different standards, he must say
that agreement among historians is not independent of
their standards. If standards influence disagreement, they
influence agreement too. So we must deny that the Relativist can exercise this option in every case of agreement
among historians as historians.

This can be put in another way. Suppose that in *every*
case in which historians agreed on judgments or an interpretation of past events, the Relativist maintained that
either (a) the historians' standards and values were irrelevant to the events in question, or (b) the historians had
the same standards and values insofar as standards and
values were relevant to their judgments about those events.
If the Relativist were to maintain this, he would thereby
not allow the possibility of a case in which historians
agreed *on the basis of* different standards and values. But
the only way in which he could rule out this possibility is
by using the occurrence of agreement and disagreement

among historians as the criterion for determining whether they have different standards and values and whether their standards and values influenced their interpretations of the past. That is, in order to determine whether two historians have the same standards and values and whether their values influence their interpretations, the Relativist would first have to determine whether they agreed on an interpretation of the past events in question. If these historians did give the same interpretation of these events, the Relativist would have to claim that they have the same standards in that respect or else that their standards were irrelevant to their interpretations. If they gave different interpretations, the Relativist would have to claim that they have different standards which did influence their interpretations. If the Relativist were to do this, then of course it would be impossible to have a case in which two historians gave the same interpretations on the basis of different standards and values. But that is only because the Relativist is deciding whether they have different standards (and whether those standards influenced their interpretations) on the basis of their giving the same or different interpretations. It is only by using this criterion that the Relativist can rule out the possibility of agreement in interpretation *on the basis of* different standards.

But the Relativist cannot use this criterion if he intends the Relativist's claim to be an informative statement about written history. To use this criterion would be similar to maintaining that rain is always preceded by the forming of cumulo-nimbus clouds on the grounds that one determines whether or not cumulo-nimbus clouds have formed by determining whether or not it has rained. This would, of course, exclude the possibility of having rain without previous formation of cumulo-nimbus clouds, but only by *defining* the expression "cumulo-nimbus clouds" as "clouds which form prior to rain." Similarly, the Relativist would be *defining* the expression "having the same standards or standards not influencing judgments" as "agreement in judgments." So the Relativist can exclude the possibility of agreement in judgments on the basis of different standards only by turning his claim into a *definition* instead of allowing it to be an informative statement about the practice of historians. Clearly, the Relativist does not want his claim to be a mere definition. He wants it to state an empirical fact about written history, since he believes that there is a causal—and hence a contingent rather than a necessary—relation between standards, values and attitudes on the one hand and particular judgments and interpretations on the other. Therefore, the Relativist must allow the possibility of agreement in judgments *on the basis of* different standards and values. I now turn to the relation between agreement in particular judgments on the basis of different standards and objectivity in history.

Suppose that historians did agree on certain particular conclusions or on interpretations, even though they held different standards and values. Why does this agreement tend to show that those judgments or interpretations are objective? The reason is this: If everyone used the same standards and values, it would not be surprising if they all reached the same conclusions. We would say, perhaps, that those conclusions could be reached *only* by using *those* standards and that *those conclusions reflected the bias inherent in the one set of standards on which they are based*. A truly objective conclusion is one that is reached on the basis of different sets of standards because, *when different standards are used, the bias inherent in one or another of these sets of standards is allowed for or eliminated*. By the use of different standards, the truth is, so to speak, "triangulated" or approached from different directions. The principle here is similar to that used when one does a mathematical problem in several different ways so as to rule out possible error made by the use of only one method. And the Relativist cannot reply to this in every case by saying that agreement would be reached in spite of the use of different standards, since, as we have seen, doing so would change his claim into a definition.

Thus, Relativists have wrongly supposed that objectivity

in history either presupposes or consists in agreement on values and standards. The highest degree of objectivity consists in agreement on particular judgments *on the basis of different standards*. This seems to be part of the concept of objectivity, that is, part of the meaning of the term "objectivity." Thus it is desirable for different historians to have different standards. Only if they use different standards can the kind of "triangulation" previously mentioned occur; if they all used the same standards, we would suspect their conclusions of being subjective for the reasons given above, even if they all agreed on those conclusions. This kind of "triangulation" achieves the same result as the use of an unbiased or impartial observer would. The Relativist would deny that there can be any unbiased or impartial observers in history, since all historians necessarily make judgments on the basis of evidence, and hence each historian necessarily uses some *one* set of standards and values. But if many different standards and values are used, all of which yield the same results, this would approach the condition of using no particular set of standards and values; that is, this would approach the situation of the unbiased or impartial observer. So this sort of "triangulation" can serve in the place of the unbiased or impartial observer. And this sort of "triangulation" seems to be at least one very important thing which can be meant by "objectivity."

The Refutation of Relativism

It would seem, then, that if historians did agree on particular judgments though they employed different standards and values, there would be good reason to say that those judgments are objective. It is not logically impossible for historians to agree in this way. It is surely at least *possible* for historians to reach such agreement—for example, for Catholic and Protestant historians to agree at some future time on an interpretation of the Reformation. And this possibility refutes both First-Level and Second

Level Relativism. First-Level Relativism denies that it is *possible* for historical judgments to be objective. But certainly it is possible for historians with different values to *agree* on particular judgments. Hence it is *possible* for particular judgments to be objective. Therefore, First-Level Relativism is unsound. Furthermore, if historians did agree on particular judgments, we would *know* that they did agree and on which judgments they agreed. Hence we would know *which* judgments were objective. Therefore, Second-Level Relativism is unsound.

As we have already seen in the case of Croce, if one already holds a Construction Theory of History, Relativism will not constitute a problem for him. But here I am considering whether or not Relativism can be used to support a Construction Theory of History. Since Relativism seems to be based on a mistaken notion of what constitutes objectivity, it does not lead to or support scepticism about knowledge of past events. Therefore Relativism cannot constitute an argument of this sort for a Construction Theory of History. Consequently, in later chapters better arguments for scepticism will be presented in order that they may serve as a basis for such a theory of the nature of the historian's activities.

PART

IV

Historical Relativism does not provide a sound basis for scepticism about historical knowledge, as the discussion in Chapter Five has shown. Therefore, in Part IV I will present and discuss five different arguments which, I believe, provide a better foundation for such scepticism. Here I will indicate briefly the nature and significance of each of these arguments, each purporting to show that a certain necessary condition of the possibility of historical knowledge is not fulfilled and cannot be fulfilled:

(1) In order to have historical knowledge, it must be possible to have evidence about the past, for historical knowledge is, by definition, knowledge the past that is based on evidence. I will try to show in Chapter Six that nothing can serve as evidence about the past, since the required correlations cannot be established. If nothing can serve as evidence about the past, historical knowledge is impossible.

(2) But in order to support the argument given in Chapter Six, it is necessary to determine whether there can be an ultimate justification of memory beliefs. The discussion in Chapter Seven is intended to give plausibility to the claim that there can be no ultimate justification of memory beliefs. This supports the argument given in Chapter Six. Perhaps more important, it shows that any procedure for finding out about the past which involves the use of memory is to that extent ultimately unjustifiable. Since it seems that any procedure used for finding out about the past would require the use of memory, another necessary condition of the possibility of historical

knowledge—namely, the justifiability of memory—is not and perhaps cannot be fulfilled.

(3) In order to have historical knowledge, propositions about the past must be meaningful. The Verification Argument, which I present and discuss in Chapter Eight, is intended to show that no proposition about the past can be meaningful. The soundness of the Verification Argument, I believe, depends on the falsity of a certain doctrine about the function of verb tenses (see pp. 152-154). If the Verification Argument is sound, yet another necessary condition of the possibility of historical knowledge—namely, the meaningfulness of propositions about the past—cannot be fulfilled.

(4) This same question—whether propositions about the past can be meaningful—is taken up again in Chapter Nine through a discussion of the possibility of acquiring the concept of the past. If it is not possible to acquire the concept of the past and if this implies that no one can have the concept of the past, it follows that no one can understand any proposition about the past. But if propositions about the past are not meaningful, there can be no historical knowledge.

(5) In order to have historical knowledge, it is necessary that the past not change. In Chapter Ten I will defend the possibility of changes in the past against an objection raised by G. E. M. Anscombe. If the past can change, then at least our knowledge of the past is very limited. And perhaps there can be no knowledge of the past if a certain theory about the meaningfulness and truth of propositions about the past is sound.

Each of these arguments is intended to provide support for a certain theory of the nature of the historian's activities. The significance of these arguments in this respect is to be discussed in Part V.

CHAPTER SIX

𐄂𐄂𐄂𐄂𐄂𐄂𐄂𐄂𐄂

CORRELATION AND EVIDENCE

Introduction

We turn in this chapter to another sort of argument for scepticism about the possibility of historical knowledge. I call this argument "The Correlation Argument." It purports to show *that there can be no evidence about past events*. If there can be no such thing as evidence about past events, then there can be no *historical* knowledge about past events, since historical knowledge of the past *is* knowledge based on evidence rather than knowledge obtained by, for instance, intuition or revelation.

The Correlation Argument

The Correlation Argument has already been mentioned in connection with Oakeshott and Collingwood. It is as follows: In order for something E to be counted as evidence for the truth of some proposition P which is about some historical event H, a correlation must first have been discovered between things (documents, ruins, artifacts, etc.) like E and events like H. *Only if such a correlation has been established is one justified in inferring from the existence of E to the existence of H.* For example, the presence of certain markings and shadows on an X-ray photograph counts as evidence for the presence of tuberculosis only because in a certain number of cases in which such markings have been observed, the patient has been found to have tuberculosis. But H is a past event and no event will be sufficiently like H to aid in establish-

ing the correlation unless it too is a past event. And the
difficulty is that *E* and things like *E* which exist in the
present cannot be correlated with *H* and events like *H*
which exist in the *past*. For in order to establish such a
correlation, one would have to know that the past events
that are similar to *H* had occurred. Therefore, one would
have to observe the past events in order to know that the
past events had occurred. How else could one know that
the past events had occurred other than by observing their
occurrence?

It might be said that one could know about the occurrence of past events by the use of evidence. But to say this
would be to beg the question, since the Correlation Argument purports to show that nothing can serve as evidence
about the past. Hence we cannot assume that there can be
evidence about events like *H*. Thus, one can know that
events like *H* occurred in the past only by directly observing those past events.

"Direct observation" of events like *H* would involve
time-travel. Such observation could take place only if the
historian were able to travel into the past and thus exist at
the moment when the event in question takes place. But
no historian can travel into the past, at least with our
present state of technological development. Hence past
events similar to *H* cannot be observed. This means that
no correlation can be established between such events and
things like *E*. Therefore, no historian can now have evidence for the occurrence of past events. A necessary condition of the possibility of such evidence is the establishment of a correlation, and a necessary condition of the
establishment of such a correlation is that the historian
directly observe past events of the type in question. But
the latter necessary condition has never been fulfilled and
cannot now be fulfilled. Hence, nothing can now serve as
evidence for the occurrence of such events.

Some have claimed that travel into the past is logically
impossible. If so, then the conclusion of this argument

would be that it is logically impossible, not just techno-logically impossible, for anything to serve as evidence about the past and hence logically impossible for historical knowledge to exist, if written history is regarded as a record or an interpretation of the past based on evidence about the past. What the historian says about the past must be based on evidence; this is what distinguishes the historian from the mystic who claims to be able to "see into the past." Since nothing can be counted as evidence about past events, and historical knowledge is knowledge about the past based on evidence about the past, there is no such thing and (if time-travel is logically impossible) can be no such thing as historical knowledge.

The Generalized Correlation Argument

The general sceptical position, of which the Cor-relation Argument is an expression, can also be put in a somewhat different and more general way. We will call this way "the Generalized Correlation Argument." In order for an event, object, document, etc., *E* to serve as evidence for the truth of some conclusion *C*, it must be known that other conclusions like *C* that have been based on other events, documents, or artifacts like *E* have been true. That is, it must be known that inferences based on things like *E* have (or would have) led to true conclusions that are like *C*. What other basis could there be for regard-ing *E* as *evidence* for *C*? This means that some conclu-sions similar to *C* have already been found to be true. One respect—perhaps the most important respect—in which they must be similar to *C* is that they must be about the past, as *C* is. Since we are again discussing the conditions under which something can be evidence, we cannot assume that the conclusions similar to *C* can be known to be true on the basis of evidence about them. The problem thus is to determine the truth or falsity of conclusions about the past apart from evidence. Since the use of evidence is not possible in this case for this reason, and since direct observation of the past is not possible, the truth or falsity of conclusions about the past cannot be determined. Thus there cannot be historical knowledge of the past.

How does the Generalized Correlation Argument differ from the Correlation Argument? First, the former is more general than the latter. The former concerns conclusions or propositions about any aspect of the past—trends, events, the motives of agents, institutions, and so on—whereas the latter concerns only conclusions about events. Second, since the Correlation Argument concerns events, the possibility of direct observation of those events will be enough to refute it. But the Generalized Correlation Argument deals with things that are not observable—at least, not in the same sense. An event can be observed, provided it is of fairly short duration and not composed of too many other events. But a change in the climate of economic opinion cannot in the same sense be observed. So the Generalized Correlation Argument cannot be refuted as easily as can the Correlation Argument.

But it must also be said that the two arguments have roughly the same form: in the Generalized Correlation Argument the putative evidence is to be correlated with true conclusions, whereas in the Correlation Argument, the putative evidence is to be correlated with the occurrence of events.

A Possible Reply to the Correlation Arguments

One reply to these sceptical arguments is that we are time travellers in the sense of travel from the present "into" the future. (This is not to say that we ever experience the future *as* the future. We always experience the future as the present, that is, as a past future.) We can thus observe correlations between past events (former present events) and present evidence. For example, we now observe that cumulo-nimbus clouds are overhead and that certain atmospheric conditions prevail; at a later time, we observe rain; and we note a fairly constant conjunction between cumulo-nimbus clouds and these atmospheric conditions on the one hand and the occurrence of rain on the other. Our established correlation enables us to predict rain at some future time. But it also enables us to make inferences about the past. For if we now observe rain, we have some (though perhaps not much) justification for saying that at some past time, certain atmospheric and cloud conditions prevailed. And, in general, if we have established a causal relationship between two types of factors, we can make inferences from putative effects to causes which give their conclusions some degree of probability. It can easily be shown that this type of situation is found in history too. A person might establish a causal relationship between certain economic conditions and the occurrence of revolutions. Then he can infer the previous existence of those conditions from the occurrence of a revolution.

Even if this sort of reply cannot justify all that the historian requires, it does show that there *can* be evidence concerning past events, and thus constitutes a refutation of the Correlation Argument since that argument is intended to show that there *cannot* be *any* such evidence.

The Correlation Argument attempts to show the impossibility of having evidence about past events. All sceptical arguments attempt to prove that something is impossible, for example, that unbiased historical knowledge is impossible. Therefore, such arguments can be refuted by proving the *possibility* of that which the sceptic claims is impossible. To use the same example, we refuted the Relativist by showing that agreement on particular issues in history is *possible*, even if it has not in fact been attained. And to refute the Correlation Argument we need only show that evidence about past events is possible, not that there actually is any such evidence. We have proved this possibility in discussing inference from effects to causes.

Use of the Argument from Analogy

Inferences from effects to causes may not give the historian enough types of possible evidence to enable him to determine very much about the past. But the range of possible evidence can be greatly expanded by use of the argument from analogy. Suppose that a historian finds that Baron X, who was in control of the government of Ruritania in 1712, had appointed Y and Z to fairly high positions in his administration. The historian believes that Y and Z were rivals of Baron X for power. But Baron X's having appointed them to positions of power seems to be evidence against this hypothesis, since if Y and Z were rivals, it appears likely that X would have attempted to prevent them from gaining power of any sort. Then the historian finds some evidence that Y and Z were members of X's own political party. The historian knows of present-day cases in which prime ministers have appointed rivals belonging to their own parties to governmental positions, in order to unify the party before it must deal with some crucial situation. Mollifying the rivals by giving them some power also gives them a stake in the continuing hegemony of the party. They will presumably now work for the party rather than only for themselves. Besides, if they are in the government, the prime minister can "keep his eye on them." The historian thus infers that Baron X probably appointed Y and Z to his government for the same reasons and that it is still plausible to regard Y and Z as rivals of X. He would then go on to look for evidence supporting the hypothesis that Baron X's party was about to face some crucial situation.

The historian was using an argument from analogy. The actions of some recent governmental leaders were similar to Baron X's action. Those leaders did what they did for a certain reason. And the historian infers that Baron X did what he did for the same reason. The important feature about this sort of inference is that it can be used to justify inferences regarding the past without requiring any prior observation of the past concerning the aspect about which the inference is made. Given that an event satisfying the description "X introduced his rivals into the government" occurred in the past, all of the evidence for the conclusion "He did it in order to create party unity" exists in the present.

But this use of the argument from analogy clearly can only *extend* the range of possible evidence about past events. It *cannot*, by itself, constitute a conclusive answer to the sceptic, since the argument from analogy can be applied only after it is known that there *did* occur some event in the past which *is* similar to one or more present events. That is, the argument from analogy can be used only after an analogy has been established between a present event and a past event (such as the action of Baron X). But establishing the existence of such an analogy cannot be done by using another argument from analogy of the same sort. An analogy must first be established before *any* argument *from* analogy can be used. To establish the analogy, one must establish that the past event has certain characteristics. It is at this point that a way of knowing about the past event other than by analogy becomes necessary. That way is inference based on correlations. The argument from analogy can be used only after correlations have been established, because these correlations provide some justification for the belief that past events that are analogous to present events did occur.

The only putative evidence we have about past events consists of such things as documents, artifacts, memoirs, and so on. And there is no reason to regard these as evidence about the past unless they, or similar items, have been correlated with past events—unless, that is, we already know that documents and artifacts do sometimes give true information about the past. We have shown that it is indeed possible to make such correlations between causes and effects. Hence it appears that the Correlation Arguments, which claimed that the establishment of such correlations is impossible, have been refuted.

Is This Refutation
of the Correlation Arguments Satisfactory?

The Correlation Arguments have apparently been refuted by claiming that causal relations can be established even if the historian cannot observe past events while they are past. The Correlation Arguments purport to show that no correlation between present facts or states of affairs and past events can ever be established, and for this reason no present states of affairs can ever be used as evidence for the occurrence of past events. The reply that we have given to this argument is that causal laws can be established and that such causal laws make probabilistic inferences from present effects to past causes possible.

But this reply is satisfactory only if the historian is justified in using memory while establishing these causal laws. The cause and the effect in each instance typically occur at different times. So the historian must remember what he observed concerning the cause while he is observing the putative effect. But is he justified in believing that his memory of the causes is accurate? If he is not justified in believing this, then he is not justified in asserting that there is a causal connection between causes of that sort and effects or events of that other sort. He may not have remembered the nature of the putative cause accurately, or he may even only seem to remember that the putative cause occurred, when in fact that putative cause did not occur at all.

Since this reply to the Correlation Arguments makes essential reference to the justified use of memory, we must determine whether the use of memory can be justified. I will take up this question in the next chapter. Only if memory beliefs can be justified is this reply to the Correlation Arguments satisfactory.

CHAPTER SEVEN

ⵀⵀⵀⵀⵀⵀⵀⵀ

THE JUSTIFICATION OF
MEMORY BELIEFS

The Problem of Justifying Memory Beliefs

If we have established a causal relationship between two types of factors, we can make probabilistic
inferences from effects to causes, as well as inferences
from causes to effects. This possibility of inferring from
effects to causes was cited in refuting scepticism about
evidence in Chapter Six. But now we must deal with a
very powerful reply (suggested in Chapter Six, p. 120)
which the sceptic might make to this attempted refutation.

The sceptic might point out that the establishment of a
causal relation involves the use of memory. The cause
occurs at an earlier time than does the effect; hence the
cause must be remembered, while the effect is being observed. But how does the observer know, while he is observing the effect, that his memory of the cause is correct?
One cannot, while observing the effect, check the accuracy
of one's memory of the cause by repeating one's observations of the cause; the cause is then "in the past" and is
inaccessible to further observation. (In this chapter the
term "memory" will be regarded as synonymous with
"memory belief" and "ostensible memory.")

The sceptic's argument has two parts, corresponding to
two theses the sceptic attempts to prove. The first thesis is:
It can be proved that some memories are incorrect. The
second thesis is: *No memory or memory belief can be
proved to be correct.* And the sceptic concludes from these
two theses that we can never know that any given memory

or memory belief is correct. He further concludes that since the historian cannot know that any memory or memory belief is correct, the historian is not justified in making use of memories or memory beliefs in establishing causal relationships. But memories must be used in establishing causal relationships because there is always an interval of time both between the observation of cause and effect and between the observations of the various instances of causation on the basis of which the correlation between cause and effect is established. And during these intervals the previous observations must be remembered. But since memory cannot be used in this way, such correlations cannot be established; thus, scepticism about the possibility of having evidence concerning the past is reinstated.

If the sceptic's argument is sound, though, its consequences are even more serious. For if the sceptic can prove that the historian cannot justifiably make use of memory, he can prove that the historian can *never* justifiably use memory, even apart from establishing causal correlations. But this in itself would support scepticism about the possibility of historical knowledge, since obviously historians must sometimes rely on their own memory beliefs. Thus the sceptic's argument concerning the possibility of justifying memory beliefs presents a serious challenge to the historian. How can the sceptic prove the two theses mentioned above?

PROOF OF THE SCEPTIC'S FIRST THESIS

In order to support the first thesis, the sceptic might say that we know that our memories are sometimes mistaken because in some cases we can check our memories against what is remembered. For example, we can check our memory of the color of a chair by going to the chair and looking at it again (provided the chair still exists). And we sometimes find in this way that our memories are incorrect.

This procedure can, of course, be used only with memories of states of objects. Although we can check our memories of past states of objects, we cannot check our memories of past events by use of this procedure. Past events are events that have now finished happening and cannot be observed in the present; hence, we cannot know whether or not memories of them are correct. We cannot, for example, check our memories of past events by comparing them with records of the past. To do this would be to beg the question at issue, since the sceptic's objection about memory is, as the preceding chapter has shown, partly an objection to the possibility of anything (including records) serving as evidence about the past. We must first establish that certain memories are correct before anything can count as such evidence. And it cannot, of course, be said that one remembers that record X is a record of event Y, since this would beg the question in another way—by assuming the correctness of the memory of that relation between the record and the event.

The opponent of the sceptic might answer that the above procedure as used by the sceptic to prove the first thesis, that is, to prove the existence of mistaken memories, is of dubious validity. Can one in fact check one's memory of the color of the chair by looking at the chair now? Presumably the color of the chair is the same color as the chair had when it was previously observed; only if it is the same color can the present observation of the chair be used to check that memory. But, the opponent would continue, how is it known that the color is the same? One would, for example, have to determine that the chair had not been repainted a different color in the meantime. And determining this would be a process taking, perhaps, a great deal of time and thus would itself involve the use of memory. But how does one know that the memories relied on during this process are accurate?

In order to cast doubt on our memories of past events, the sceptic must prove that memories are in fact sometimes incorrect. And his example of the memory of the chair's color was supposed to prove this. But the sceptic's opponent is now claiming that proving a memory to be incorrect involves reliance on other memories which, if the sceptic is right about the incorrectness of some memories, cannot be assumed to be correct. But if it cannot be assumed that the memories used in this process are correct, then the process itself has no value as a proof or part of a proof of the incorrectness of the original memory. If the sceptic is right, then the sceptic has given a proof that is susceptible to his own scepticism; thus his proof is not a proof after all. He cannot both be right about the untrustworthiness of memories and at the same time try to prove the untrustworthiness of memories by relying on certain memories. Thus, his opponent would say, the sceptic cannot prove his first thesis. The sceptic cannot prove that some memories are incorrect and, hence, cannot cast doubt in this way on the correctness of all memories, including memories of past events.

However, I believe that this argument does not succeed in showing the sceptic's proof of his first thesis to be unsound, for he can offer his opponent the following dilemma (which we will call "Dilemma *M*"): if the memories used in the above process involving the chair are correct, the memory of the color of the chair is proved to be incorrect; if the memories used in the process are incorrect, it follows that some memories are incorrect, namely those used in the process; either the memories used in the process are correct or else they are incorrect; and in either case some memories are incorrect. This proves the sceptic's first thesis.

The proof (Dilemma *M*) just given partly takes the form of showing that the correctness of one memory or set of memories is incompatible with the correctness of another memory. Incompatibility among memories has been used by others to prove that memory in general is not absolutely certain. If it could be proved that every memory is correct, then the sceptic could not raise his objection. But C. I. Lewis, for example, says: "The assumption of certainty for memory in general would be contradicted by the fact that we remember remembering things and later finding them to be false."[1] Apparently Lewis is suggesting the following: One remembers now (memory X) that another memory (memory Y) turned out to be incorrect; then another dilemma (which we will call "Dilemma L") results, for if memory X is correct, then memory Y is incorrect, and if memory X is incorrect, then a memory (namely X itself) is incorrect; but either memory X is correct or it is incorrect; and in either case some memory is incorrect. But Lewis' argument in defense of the sceptic is not sound when taken by itself. Notice that the first horn of Dilemma L is: "If memory X is correct, then memory Y is incorrect." According to this, what is *remembered* is that memory Y *is* incorrect. This assumes that the person could find at some previous time that memory Y was incorrect since he now remembers that memory Y was *in fact* incorrect. But this is precisely what the sceptic's opponent claims is not possible. The sceptic's opponent claims that one cannot find out whether a given memory is incorrect, for attempting to prove a memory incorrect itself requires the use of memory. Lewis assumes that it is possible to have found out that memory Y was incorrect, for only if one had found this out could one later truly remember that memory Y was incorrect. The sceptic's opponent denies this assumption. Hence Lewis' dilemma does not prove that some memories are incorrect.

PROOF OF THE SCEPTIC'S SECOND THESIS

But the argument I have given (Dilemma M) does seem to prove that some memories are incorrect. So let us assume that the sceptic has proved this first thesis. How can he prove his second thesis: that no memory can be proved to be correct? Because some memories *are* incorrect, any memory *could be* incorrect; hence, before a certain memory can be relied on by the historian, that memory must be proved to be correct. There are two restrictions on such proofs of correctness. (1) The proof cannot involve direct observation of the past event of which the memory purports to be a memory, since if the event could be observed, it would be present rather than past.[2] It might be objected that it is not logically impossible for someone to build a machine that allows one to observe past events, a type of television apparatus that could show past events on its screen. Such a machine is perhaps not logically impossible. But the existence of such a machine would not answer the sceptic's argument. For how would we know that the machine was giving us a direct look at *past* events rather than at future events? And even if we did know that we were observing past events, how would we know that the machine was rendering those events correctly? In order to know that its renditions were correct, we would have to have some *other* way of knowing about those past events. And if we did have another way of knowing about past events, we would not need the machine. (2) The proof of the correctness of an individual memory cannot involve the use of other memories that have not already been proved to be correct. If the proof employed memories that were not correct, the proof would not be a proof. But there are memories used in all ostensible proofs that have more than one step. The earlier steps in the proofs have to be remembered while the later steps are being considered. Therefore, it would first have to be proved that the memories used in those proofs are correct. But this would also involve the use of memories. This procedure leads to a vicious infinite regress. Hence a proof having more than one step cannot be used to prove the correctness of a memory.

How, then, *are* these memories to be proved correct? Since direct observation (a method of proof having, so to speak, one step) and the use of proofs having more than one step are both ruled out—and since the use of evidence about past events is not yet possible, for reasons already given—there seems to be no way in which such memories can be proved correct. Therefore no memories can be proved correct. But since some memories can be proved incorrect, as Dilemma M establishes, and no memory can be proved correct, the historian is not justified in relying on *any* memory whatsoever, since any memory whatsoever may be incorrect. This is, of course, a very serious restriction for the historian. We have seen that the existence of evidence about the past depends on the establishment of correlations which in turn depends on the use of memory. Thus it follows that no such correlations can be established, and hence nothing can count as evidence about the past.

This type of scepticism about memory is quite different from a certain type of scepticism about the reality of the past. Scepticism about memory says, in effect: Memories cannot be known to give reliable information about the past. Scepticism about the reality of the past says, in effect: There are no past events at all and, hence, no knowledge about them. These two types of scepticism are closely related, however. Scepticism about memory assumes that there are such things as past events and concerns their correct representation by memories. It does not deny that there can be veridical memories. This form of scepticism does not claim that all memories *are* incorrect, but only that we cannot know whether they are correct or incorrect. But scepticism about the reality of the past is one type of scepticism about the existence of any veridical memories at all. A memory is always about something in the past. Therefore if there are no past events or past states of affairs, there cannot be any correct memories. That there is no past entails that there are no correct memories, although the latter proposition does not entail the former.

The Coherence Theory

At this point it will be said that absolute certainty about memories is not required in order for the use of memories by the historian to be justifiable. If it can be shown that some memories are *very probably* correct, such memories can be justifiably used.

But what could show that there is a high degree of probability that a given memory is correct? In fact, what could show that it is probable to *any* degree that a given memory is correct? We speak of probability in connection with evidence: such-and-such evidence renders a certain proposition probable to this or that degree. But there cannot be such evidence in the case of memories, because memory would have to be used in gathering such evidence. Is there any way of assigning degrees of probability to memory beliefs that does not depend on the use of evidence?

There is one aspect of memories that has been used for this purpose, namely, the "coherence" of a memory with other memories and with present observations. Consider the following examples:

(1) Jones passes a man on the street. The man looks vaguely familiar and Jones tries to remember who he is. Jones is sure that the man's last name begins with "S," that he is British and an economist, and that he last saw the man in Singapore. Jones tries to remember when he was last in Singapore. He believes that it was in 1953 during his employment by a UN economic development agency. Gradually Jones brings back details of the two months he spent in Singapore. Finally he remembers that the man he passed is named Smith and that he was in 1953 the economic attaché at the British Consulate in Singapore.

(2) Green is visiting Brown. Green notices a painting on the wall and says to Brown: "That's the painting you bought in London when we were both there, isn't it?" Green goes on to describe the auction, their other activities during the visit, and so on, all of which are confirmed by Brown. Brown later shows Green several letters from friends in London that mention their trip.

These two examples illustrate two types of coherence theories. One type of theory holds that a memory is justifiably regarded as probably correct if it "coheres" with or "fits" with *other memories*, just as Jones's memories of Smith's name and position fit together with his memories of his sojourn in Singapore in 1953. The second type of theory holds that a memory is justifiably regarded as probably correct if it "coheres" with *present observations*, just as Green's memories of the painting and the visit to London fit together with Brown's remarks and the letters from their London friends. And, of course, there is a third type of theory, a composite of the first two, which holds that a memory is justifiably regarded as probably correct if it coheres with both other memories and present observations.

The first type of view has one advantage over the second. Many memories are such that they have no relation to present observations or experiences. For example, one may seem to remember the pair of shoes one wore to a Presidential Inauguration five years ago, but as there are no photographs of the occasion, no one else now claims to remember the pair, and so on, no present observations can be said to cohere with that memory (if "coherence" means more than merely lack of conflict). But one may have other memories that cohere with this memory—memories of the occasion on which one bought those shoes, of comments by one's secretary on the shoes, how long they lasted, other occasions on which they were worn, and so on. Thus the first type of theory can show that this memory is justifiably regarded as probably correct, but the second type cannot. If we do in fact believe that this memory is justifiably so regarded, then the first theory is more adequate than the second as an account of our beliefs about memory. Conversely, there may be memories that cohere with present observations but with which there are no other memories for it to cohere; the second type of theory would be superior to the first with respect to these memories. Since the third type of theory can handle both sorts of cases, it may seem preferable to either of the first two types. But the third type is a combination of the first two and, hence, will be sound only if the first two types are sound. Thus we will examine each of the first two types. And what we require is not a theory that accounts for our beliefs about the justification of memory, but a theory on the basis of which memories can, in fact, be justified. We may believe that a memory is justifiably regarded as probably correct if it coheres with something else. But is this belief correct? Does coherence in fact provide this sort of justification?

Let us consider the first type of theory. Why does coherence with other memories show that a given memory is probably correct? After all, suppose those other memories are not themselves correct; certainly, coherence with them would tend to show, if anything, that the given memory was incorrect rather than correct. So we must first know whether or not those other memories are correct. But how are we to determine this—by their coherence with still other memories? The same problem will then arise concerning the correctness of *those* memories. In view of this seemingly infinite regress, how can coherence with other memories provide justification?

C. I. Lewis claims that a certain type of coherence relation—which he calls "congruence"—can provide justification. His theory is, in fact, an example of the third type of coherence theory, since he speaks of the congruence of memories "with one another and with present sense experience"; but since he evidently does not feel that "present sense experience" has a different function here from that of other memories, we can at first treat his view as an example of the first type of theory.[3] Lewis agrees that mere consistency with other memories does not increase the probability that the given memory is correct. "The mere relationship of consistency amongst statements believed—the fact that, together, they constitute a completely self-consistent system—provides by itself no ground whatever for rational credence in any one of them."[4] The reason for this, according to Lewis, is: "Every empirical supposition, being a contingent statement, is contained in some self-consistent system which is as comprehensive as you please."[5] That is, given any false statement or incorrect memory belief, there will be some system with which it is consistent. Hence, such consistency provides no evidence of truth or correctness.

Lewis proposes a stronger relation, congruence, in place of mere consistency: "A set of statements, or a set of supposed facts asserted, will be said to be congruent if and only if they are so related that the antecedent probability of any one of them will be increased if the remainder of the set can be assumed as given premises."[6] As Lewis' examples show, this can be stated in a broader way: If any subset of a congruent set of statements is found to be true, the probability of the remaining statements' being true is increased over what it was before this was found to be the case. This is certainly not the case for a merely consistent set of statements: "Cloves are grown in India" and "Some cosmic rays are generated in the upper atmosphere" are consistent with each other, and yet the truth of one does not increase the probability of the other. It is also true that the strongest such relation among statements is the entailment of the remaining statements by any subset of statements; and congruence, though stronger than consistency, is not as strong as this.

Lewis seems to claim that if a memory is a member of a congruent set of memories, the probability of its correctness is high. But he does not state the characteristics which indicate that a certain set of statements is a congruent set. He does not state how to tell when the truth of a given set of statements increases the probability of another statement's being true. What he does is give examples of congruent sets. He cites the piecing together of facts by a detective in building a case against a suspect or by a scientist in constructing a scientific theory. He also cites the following set:

'H' = "This pack of cards has never been shuffled."

'K' = "Cards are packed at the factory in the order: extra card, king of hearts, queen of hearts, and so on; suits being in the order hearts, clubs, diamonds, spades."

'C_1' = "The first card dealt will be the extra card."

'C_2' = "The second card dealt will be the king of hearts" . . .

'C_{15}' = "The fifteenth card dealt will be the king of clubs" . . .[7]

It is true that we would regard this as a congruent set. If K, C_1, and C_2 are found to be true, the probabilities of C_{15} and H are increased over their antecedent probabilities.

Apparently what we must do to determine if a set is congruent is find whether or not we believe that the probability of any member is related in the required way to the truth of the other members. Of course, to find this out is to perform a process that takes a certain amount of time and, therefore, involves the use of memory. At time t_1 the person may decide that the truth of K and C_1 would increase the probability of H. At a later time, t_2, he may decide that the truth of K, C_1, and C_2 will also increase the probability of H. But at t_2 he will also have to remember that at t_1 he made a certain decision about the relation between K, C_1, and H. But how does he know at t_2 that this memory of his decision at t_1 is correct? Presumably this memory would have to be found to be a member of a congruent set also. But determining that it is a member of such a set would take time and, hence, also involve other memories in a similar way. These memories would then have to be checked for congruence relations. Thus, this procedure leads to a vicious infinite regress. Because of this regress, it could never be determined that the first memory was a member of a congruent set. Even if the person kept a record of his previous computations, he would have to remember such things as that he (or some other reliable person) made the record.

The second difficulty with Lewis' theory as a theory of the first type is that the examples he gives of congruent sets are not sufficiently similar to a set consisting wholly of memory beliefs. The sets he cites contain statements that *are* known to be true. The detective knows certain facts about the kidnapping. The scientist knows what the results of certain experiments are. But a set consisting *solely* of memory beliefs does not contain any propositions *known* to be true. If the sceptic is right, *all* the memory beliefs in the set are dubitable and none are known to be true. Hence if congruent sets must contain propositions known to be true in order to be congruent, no set consisting solely of memory beliefs can be a congruent set.

But perhaps a set need not contain statements known to be true in order to be congruent; for the set H, K, C_1, C_2, C_{15} does not contain any such statements. But although this may allow a set of memory beliefs to be congruent, another difficulty arises. If a congruent set does not contain any statements *known* to be true, the probability of any other member of the set is not increased. A congruent set is such that *if* any member were found out to be true, *then* the probability of the remaining members *would be* increased. But unless we *know* that some members are true, we are not justified in attributing an increased probability to the other members merely on the basis of their being members of a congruent set. That they are members of a congruent set means only that they are *in a position* to have an increased probability attributed to them. Merely being members of a congruent set does not by itself increase the probability of statements one iota. We must in addition know that some members of the set *are* in fact true. But *none* of the members of the set consisting wholly of memory beliefs is already *known* to be true. Hence, although this set is a congruent set, none of its members can be regarded as gaining an increase in probability. Of course, *if* some members of this set can be known to be true, *then* other members will be more probable than they otherwise are. So in order for Lewis' method to work, there must be some *other* method of determining if some memories are correct. But the sceptic seems to have shown that no other method is possible. And if no other method is possible, then Lewis' method cannot be used.

There is a way of introducing statements known to be

true into the set of memory beliefs. This way consists in introducing statements about present experiences as members of the set. And the necessity for doing this proves that present experiences do not play the same role in the set as do memory beliefs, even though Lewis seems to believe that they do. Statements about present experiences *must* be included in order to provide the set with statements *known* to be true. But now Lewis' theory must be examined as a theory of the second type: Memories are rendered probable by their congruence with present experiences.

The first difficulty remains, however. The process of ascertaining congruence relations among statements takes time and, hence, requires the use of memory. This would seem to lead to an infinite regress of the sort previously described.

But this second type of theory involves an even more serious difficulty. Do the memory beliefs in our second example concerning Green and Brown stand in *congruence* relations to Green's present experiences? Does the fact that Green's friend has the painting hanging on his wall make it more probable that Green's memory belief about the auction is correct? Might not his friend just as probably have bought the painting in a private sale from a dealer? His friend did say that he bought the painting at the auction, but might not the friend be lying? In fact, couldn't Green have just those experiences he is now having and yet his memory of the auction be incorrect? Green remembers that Brown bought the painting at an auction. Green also has the following experiences: He sees the painting on Brown's wall, and he hears Brown say that he bought the painting at an auction. It is not clear that these statements stand in congruence relations. And yet the Green–Brown case is typical of the situations in which Lewis' theory would be applied.

We do believe that there is some sort of relation between Green's memory and Brown's having the picture on his wall and saying what he did say. To express this relationship, we must introduce still other statements: (a) people who buy paintings usually hang them on their walls rather than giving them away or selling them immediately; (b) people generally do not lie to their friends. Only if (a) and (b) are known to be true can Green's present experiences add probability to his memory of the auction. Present experiences *by themselves* do not do so. But how do we know that (a) and (b) are true? These are empirical propositions which we come to believe to be true in the course of our experience in the world. Many such empirical beliefs are involved in the assignment of probabilities to one statement on the basis of other statements. But these empirical beliefs are generalizations; they concern the way in which people and objects usually behave. Thus they are based on various observations of particular cases of behavior. But in order to know that the generalizations are justifiable, one must *remember* at least some of these particular cases or that there were such cases. One must thus have certain memory beliefs. But are *those* memory beliefs justifiably to be regarded as correct? They are, according to Lewis, only if they too stand in congruence relations with some present experiences. But ascertaining whether or not *these* congruence relations do exist will involve reference to other empirical generalizations and hence to other memories. This clearly leads to another vicious infinite regress.

Thus Lewis' theory when viewed as a theory of the second type is unsound. And since his theory is unsound when viewed as being of the first type and of the second type, it cannot be sound when viewed as a theory of the third type, since the third is a conjunction of the first two.

Our Beliefs about Memory

So far we have been assuming that ultimately we have only one source of knowledge about the past. Even the reports of eyewitnesses are dependent on the use of memory, for those reports are typically spoken or written after the events reported have occurred. But perhaps scepticism about memory could be eliminated if (1) there were some way of knowing about the past that did not ultimately depend on memory, or (2) some memories were immediately certain and thus require no justification. We must next examine a theory that can be characterized as making either of these claims. For it holds that some statements about the past are absolutely certain. So if the sceptic claims that all memories are dubitable, the holder of this theory can admit this and yet maintain that there is a way of obtaining certain knowledge about the past that does not depend on memory. On the other hand, if the sceptic says that memory is ultimately the only source of knowledge about the past, the holder of this theory can admit this and claim that some memory beliefs—namely, those expressed in these statements about the past—are absolutely certain.

What statements about the past would the holder of this theory regard as absolutely certain? He would claim that the following would be regarded as absolutely certain by those who made them and who regard them as true at all: "I was alive two months ago," "I saw the sun rise this morning," "I attended Columbia University," "I travelled in Europe several years ago," and so on. Most of the statements about the past which would be regarded by a given person as certain are statements about the person's own past experiences. But whatever statements these are, they would be regarded as certain for the same reason: no evidence could prove them to be false.

Why is it that no evidence could prove them to be false? These statements are contingent statements; that is, they are statements that might have been false, even if they are in fact true. Thus, they are not like such statements as "Every circle has a center." This latter statement cannot be proven false by evidence, because evidence is not relevant to it. There can be no evidence against this statement since one cannot discover a circle without a center. But there can be no evidence *for* this statement either. A suc-

cessful search for circles with centers would not increase
the probability of this statement one bit. This statement is
true in virtue of the meanings of its component words, not
in virtue of the state of the world. Hence evidence, which
results from investigations into the state of the world, cannot affect the probability of this statement.

Yet the statements about the past that are supposed to
be absolutely certain are not statements of this kind. As
previously noted, they are contingent: they may be true
but they might have been false. Thus they are not true in
virtue of the meanings of their component words. These
statements differ from "Every circle has a center" in another (though closely related) way also—namely, these
statements express *propositions* for or against which there
can be evidence. Jones may believe that he was in Europe
several years ago. If Jones does believe this, no evidence
can count for or against the statement "I was in Europe
several years ago," *insofar as Jones is concerned.* But the
statement "I was in Europe several years ago" when made
by Jones has the same meaning as the statement "Jones
was in Europe several years ago" when said by Smith. So
these two *statements* express the same *proposition.* Yet
there can be evidence for or against Smith's statement.
Smith might consider a photograph of Jones standing in
the Piazza San Marco or a newspaper interview Jones
purportedly gave in Rome as evidence for this proposition;
and he might consider a statement by Jones's wife that
Jones had never been in Europe as being evidence against
this proposition. Because there can be evidence for or
against Smith's statement, there can be evidence *for Smith*
for or against the proposition expressed by that statement.
But this proposition is much different in this respect from
the proposition expressed as "Every circle has a center."
For there can be no evidence *for anyone* for or against this
latter proposition.

The statement "I was in Europe several years ago"
differs from the statement "Every circle has a center" in
(a) being contingent, and (b) expressing a proposition for

or against which there can be evidence for some people. But both are absolutely certain, the former for the person who utters it and who believes that what he says is true and the latter for everyone. Since these two statements differ in fundamental ways, even though both are certain, each statement is certain for a different reason. "Every circle has a center" is certain because of the definitions of its component terms. But this is not why "I was in Europe several years ago" is certain for some people. The latter is certain because those who utter it while believing it to be true will not allow it to be false. These people will accept nothing as evidence against statements of these sorts. There are statements which all of us regard in this way. The implications of a person's coming to regard a statement of this sort as false are quite drastic. To claim in good faith to have gone to Europe several years ago and subsequently to come to believe that one was wrong in so claiming is to raise a possibility far more serious than a mere error in remembering. That one was in Europe several years ago is just the sort of thing that a person does not forget. In fact, more than the possibility of amnesia is at stake. A person's memories of the important or very recent events in his life constitute one of the factors that make him the person he is. Memories constitute one of the criteria for personal identity. And with such important matters as personal identity at stake, it is not surprising that a person will not allow these memory beliefs to be falsified—why, that is, he will prefer an alternative account of any evidence that might otherwise tend to show that these beliefs are false.

These absolutely certain beliefs about the past can be used to support other memory beliefs. If a person says: "I remember that St. Paul's was still standing after the Blitz," and his statement is challenged, he may reply: "I was in London in 1942." The latter statement is certain and gives some support to the former, that is, increases its probability by some degree. It is certainly not the case that, given any memory belief or any belief about the past, there is an absolutely certain statement that gives that belief some increased amount of probability. But the sceptic denies that *any* memory belief can be probable to any degree at all. So if at least one such belief can be given some degree of probability, the sceptic will have been refuted. And some memory beliefs seemingly can be given some degree of probability in the way just illustrated.

For each person there are certain memory beliefs that person regards as absolutely certain, namely, certain beliefs about his own past experiences. Does this fact show the sceptic to be wrong? The sceptic would probably deny that it does. He would say that this theory gives a correct description of what we do say about memory beliefs, how we do try to justify them, and so on. But although this may be what, in fact, we do, that we do it does not prove that what we do is justified. That a person will allow nothing to count as evidence against a certain memory belief does not prove that belief to be correct. A person's belief that he was in Europe several years ago is correct if and only if he *was* in Europe several years ago. How he regards that belief is not relevant to its correctness or incorrectness.

The sceptic would contend that this theory does not refute him but, instead, shows that he is right after all. If the above is a correct description of what we do, it shows that memory beliefs cannot ultimately be justified. Thus, what we do is make certain assumptions—we assume that certain statements about the past are correct—and give relative justification to other memory beliefs on the basis of these statements. But ultimate justification cannot be given unless these statements themselves can be justified. There are good reasons, as shown above, for assuming these rather than other statements to be true. But that these statements have been assumed to be true does not prove that they are true. The sceptic's position thus shows that certain assumptions must be made if there is to be any justification of empirical beliefs at all. Further, his position shows what some of these assumptions are, namely, certain beliefs about one's own past experiences.

Scepticism and Memory Beliefs

Neither of the two ways of justifying memory beliefs which were discussed in the previous sections of this chapter provide an ultimate justification (as opposed to a relative justification) of those beliefs. Consequently, the reply to the Correlation Arguments given in Chapter Six (pp. 116–117) is unsatisfactory. That reply depended on the possibility of establishing causal laws which, in turn, depends on the possibility of justifiably using memory. But what has been said in this chapter tends to show that the use of memory cannot ultimately be justified. Therefore, to the extent that that reply does depend on the possibility of justifiably using memory, it is unsatisfactory. Thus, the Correlation Arguments may still provide a basis for scepticism about historical knowledge.

But what has been said in this chapter also supports another sort of scepticism. It supports scepticism about any of the historian's activities that involve the use of memory—not just the activity of establishing causal relations. And this may cast doubt on the adequacy of any theory of history according to which the historian makes essential use of memory. (It should be said that these problems concerning the justification of memory are not peculiar to history. They are problems that arise in relation to any essential use of memory.)

One cannot reply to the sceptic by saying that his position rules out any possibility of ultimate justification of memory beliefs. This "reply" is merely a reiteration of the sceptic's own position. But a reply could perhaps take the form of asserting that the past is what we make of it in the present or what we believe it to be on the basis of present experiences, regardless of whether or not these beliefs correspond to the past. Present experiences would then serve as "criteria" or conclusive determinants of the truth or falsity of statements (including those based on memory) about the past. Hence memory beliefs could be determined to be true or false on the basis of present experiences.

This type of reply to the sceptic can be made by the Constructionist. The Constructionist says that since the past (or at least the historical past) *is* what is made of it by historians in the present, historians are not trying to discover or record which past events did or did not occur. The use of memory in history must be ultimately justifiable only if one is trying to discover or record what happened in the past. On the Construction Theory of History, however, the historian is trying to form a coherent whole out of present states of affairs and present beliefs about the past. Consequently, it is no objection to the Construction Theory of History to say that memory beliefs may be false. A memory belief is false owing to its lack of correspondence with past events. But on the Construction Theory of History, the historian is not concerned with "what really happened." Therefore, the lack of ultimate justification of memory beliefs does not constitute an objection to this theory of history.

CHAPTER EIGHT

𒀸𒀸𒀸𒀸𒀸𒀸𒀸𒀸𒀸

VERIFICATION AND
MEANINGFULNESS

Introduction

Thus far in Part IV we have been considering various conditions that must be fulfilled if historical knowledge is to be possible. In order for historical knowledge to be possible, it must be possible to have evidence about the past, for historical knowledge is, by definition, knowledge of the past based on evidence. In order for historical knowledge to be possible, it must be possible to provide an ultimate justification of memory. And the arguments given in the preceding chapters of Part IV are intended to show that neither of these necessary conditions of the possibility of historical knowledge is fulfilled.

In this chapter and in Chapter Nine we turn to another necessary condition of knowledge of the past, namely, that statements or propositions about the past be meaningful. If no statement or proposition about the past is meaningful, then if there is or can be historical knowledge, such knowledge is not expressible in statements or propositions. But it is very implausible to assert that there can be historical knowledge that *cannot* be expressed in statements or propositions. Consequently, if no proposition about the past is or can be meaningful, there can be no historical knowledge.

In the first section we will discuss the Verification Argument, which purports to show that no proposition about the past is or can be meaningful. The sections that follow are devoted to possible replies to the Verification

Argument. But, as I try to show in the final section of this chapter, these replies can succeed in refuting the Verification Argument only if a certain dubious doctrine about the tenses of verbs is true.

The Verification Argument

The Verification Argument is based on the principle that in order for a proposition *C* to be meaningful, *C* must be verifiable or falsifiable. That is, *C* is meaningful only if it is possible to determine whether *C* is true or false. Several varieties of this position should be distinguished: (1) *C* itself must be verifiable or falsifiable in principle; (2) *C* itself must be verifiable or falsifiable in practice; (3) propositions like *C* must be verifiable or falsifiable in principle; (4) propositions like *C* must be verifiable or falsifiable in practice. We will discuss only (1) here.

Why is it maintained that propositions are meaningful if and only if they themselves are verifiable or falsifiable in principle? This is best explained in terms of falsifiability. To say that a given proposition *P* is unfalsifiable is to say that no observations or other sorts of grounds would show it to be false. An unfalsifiable proposition would therefore have no connections with experience. Such a proposition could play no role in empirical inquiry, since it would be compatible with any state of affairs in the empirical world. Any statement that is compatible with every empirical state of affairs simply does not contain any reference to *any* such state of affairs. It cannot be used by anyone to convey information about the empirical world. For in telling someone that something is the case, one is implying that certain other things are not the case. Hence, any statement whose use does not carry this implication is not a statement that can be used to say what is the case. And every statement compatible with any state of affairs whatsoever—that is, which is unfalsifiable—obviously does not carry this implication. The statement "All bachelors are male" is compatible with every state of affairs. But it is true in virtue of the definition of the term "bachelor" and not in virtue of the existence of some state of affairs in the way that the statement "New York is east of Chicago" is. Hence, if one knows that the statement "All bachelors are male" is true, one does not thereby know that one state of affairs rather than another exists. Such statements do not rule out the existence of any state of affairs. Hence, unfalsifiable statements (such as "All bachelors are male") cannot be used to give information about any state of affairs. Therefore such statements are not meaningful: They have no empirical or descriptive meaning.

For a statement to be meaningful, it must be falsifiable. This position about meaningfulness, as it applies to statements about the past, can be put in the following way: (1) the verifiability or falsifiability of an empirical statement P is a necessary and sufficient condition of the meaningfulness of P; (2) if P is a statement about the past, it is a statement which asserts that one state of affairs has existed at a certain time rather than some other state of affairs; so it is intended as an empirical or descriptive statement rather than as, for example, a statement which is true in virtue of a definition; therefore, P is meaningful only if it is verifiable or falsifiable; (3) but if P is a statement about a past event, then P is not verifiable or falsifiable, even in principle, for the historian cannot return to the past and observe the verifying or falsifying state of affairs if such a state existed; yet only such observations could verify or falsify P; for no *evidence* could conclusively show P to be true or false; such evidence could at most show P to be probable or improbable; (4) by steps (1), (2) and (3), statements about the past are not meaningful; (5) hence, by the argument in the previous section, historical knowledge is not possible. I will call the argument consisting of propositions (1) through (5) "the Verification Argument."

The First Possible Reply to the Verification Argument: The Historian Might Have Existed in the Past

One possible reply to the Verification Argument is that the historian could have verified or falsified the statement P himself. It is assumed in this first reply that statement P must be verifiable or falsifiable in principle *by the person for whom* P *is to be meaningful*. That is why it is specified in this reply that it is the historian himself who performs the verification or falsification. So, for example, if P is about the Battle of Agincourt, one who made this reply to the Verification Argument would claim that it is logically possible that the historian might have existed at the time of the Battle of Agincourt. Hence statements made now by that historian about the Battle of Agincourt would be meaningful to that historian. But in this reply, it is being claimed that it is *now* the case that the historian could have existed at the time of the event in question. That is, it is claimed that it is now logically possible for the historian to exist at some past time. But this assumes that time-travel into the past is logically possible. Yet there are reasons for believing that such time-travel is not logically possible. Thus this reply is implausible to the extent that the arguments for the logical impossibility of time-travel are plausible.

The proponent of this first reply would probably answer this objection as follows: "The only reason why time-travel must be logically possible is because you are supposing the historian to be existing in the present; but the possibility being contemplated in this reply is not the possibility of a present-day historian actually travelling into the past; rather, the possibility being contemplated is that the present-day historian could have existed in the past *rather than* existing now; thus there would be no need for time-travel and your argument that time-travel might be logically impossible does not cast doubt on this reply."

Is it logically possible that the historian might have existed at the time of the Battle of Agincourt rather than

now? It might be objected that this is not logically possible
because the historian who exists in the past would not be
the same person as the historian who exists now, unless
the former could have had the same memories as the latter.
And if the historian existed then, he could not possibly
have the same memories as does the historian who exists
now. For the events the historian who exists now remembers *did not happen* until after the Battle of Agincourt and
hence they could not be remembered at the time of the
Battle of Agincourt by the historian who exists at the time
of that battle. Hence the same historian who exists now
could not exist at the time of that battle. However, it is
logically possible that the events the historian who exists
now remembers *might have* occurred prior to the Battle
of Agincourt. And it follows from this that it is logically
possible that the historian at the time of Agincourt might
have had those memories. And this seems to establish that
it is logically possible that the historian who exists now
might have existed at the time of Agincourt. Hence statements about Agincourt by the historian who exists now
would be meaningful to him now. So far, then, this reply
does seem to refute the Verification Argument.

The Second Possible Reply
to the Verification Argument:
Could Past Events Have Existed in the Present?

The second reply to the Verification Argument
agrees with the first reply in holding that it is the person
for whom *P* is to be meaningful who must be able in
principle to verify or falsify *P*. The second reply is that it
is logically possible that the Battle of Agincourt might
have occurred today. Hence it is logically possible that the
historian might have observed that battle and, hence, have
verified or falsified statements like *P* about that battle.

Let us suppose that the Battle of Agincourt could have
occurred today. How does this show that statements about
that battle as it occurred in the past are now meaningful?

If the battle did exist today, then presumably it would not also be a past event. So the verification or falsification would pertain to a present event, not to a past event. Thus, how does the possibility of verification or falsification with respect to a present event make statements about that event as a *past* event meaningful? It will be replied that the pastness of an event is not an essential characteristic of the event and, hence, that verification or falsification of statements about the present Battle of Agincourt would constitute verification or falsification of statements about the past Battle of Agincourt. But then we may ask what the essential characteristics of the battle are. Is the Battle of Agincourt merely a battle in which certain persons participated, in which a certain number of people were killed, which took place at a certain geographical location, and so on? Or is it also a battle that was the effect of certain trends, social forces, and events which preceded it, and that was the cause or the partial cause of various other events and states of affairs?

Surely both of these sorts of properties are properties of the Battle of Agincourt. But if the battle has both sorts of properties, how is it to be determined which properties of these two sorts are essential? If only properties of the first sort are essential, then perhaps the Battle of Agincourt could have taken place tomorrow, since, for example, it is logically possible that the participants in that battle could have been alive tomorrow. But if properties of the second sort are essential, then it is doubtful whether the battle could have taken place tomorrow. For properties of the second sort are such as to essentially involve a certain temporal "location." For example, if the Battle of Agincourt is partly the effect of certain other events, then it *necessarily* must occur after those events; and if it is the partial cause of still other events, then it *necessarily* must precede those other events. So if that battle were to occur in the present (let us say at time t_1), the events which are the partial causes or are partly the effects of that battle would also have to occur at different times from those at which they did, in fact, occur. The times of their supposed occurrence would have to have the same relations to t_1 as their actual times of occurrence do have to the actual time of occurrence of the Battle of Agincourt. And if all events are part of an extremely large net of causal relations, as seems quite likely, then to have the Battle of Agincourt occur at time t_1 would result in the whole series of the events which have occurred in the world being moved "forward" (toward t_1) along the world time line. The net result would be that we would merely call the time of occurrence of the Battle of Agincourt "t_1." But this would not be to have the Battle of Agincourt occur in *the present*, since the event of the birth of our historian has also been moved in the same way "forward" along the time line; the present for our historian is now six centuries forward from t_1. "The present" is the time at which our historian is living, not some time merely called 1965. Thus, the Battle of Agincourt cannot be moved into the present without moving the present still farther on along the world time line. This would leave everything just as it is now.

It may be objected that properties of the second sort are not essential properties of the battle. But if it is claimed that they are not, some proof must be offered for that thesis. Such a proof must involve a criterion of what is to count as an essential property. And if these properties are not essential properties, then a battle that occurred tomorrow in the correct location and which had the same participants as the Battle of Agincourt dressed in exactly the same way and using exactly the same weapons would count as the Battle of Agincourt. This seems implausible. It seems more plausible that *every* property of an event is an essential property of that event. Of course, if this is true, then the second reply to the Verification Argument is unsound, since the temporal "location" of an event is an essential property of the event, and thus no event could change its temporal "location" and remain the same event.

If not every property of an event is an essential property

of that event, then perhaps properties of the second sort are not essential properties of the Battle of Agincourt. And if they are not essential properties, then the second reply to the Verification Argument would so far be sound.

The Third Possible Reply to the Verification Argument: Possible Verification or Falsification by Someone Other Than the Historian

Let us now consider a third possible reply to the sceptic. Notice that proposition (2) of the Verification Argument implies that P must be falsifiable by the historian himself, if P is to be meaningful. The first and second replies to the Verification Argument assume that this is necessary if P is to be meaningful. But is it in fact necessary that it be possible for the *historian* to falsify P in order for P to be meaningful? After all, if P is meaningful, it is not meaningful for the historian or for some particular person and not for other particular persons. If P is meaningful at all, it is meaningful for everyone. So there seems to be no reason why P has to be falsifiable by a particular such as the historian. If P is falsifiable by someone, then P is falsifiable. And if P is falsifiable, then P is meaningful. So if P is falsifiable by someone, then P is meaningful for everyone. Although P may not, even in principle, be falsifiable by a certain person—namely, the historian—it may be falsifiable by some other person. And if there is at least one person for which P is falsifiable, then we can say without qualification that P is falsifiable. This is true regardless of the temporal status of the subject matter of P. If P is about some past event E, then the observing of E or of some state of affairs incompatible with the occurrence of E by *some* past person will satisfy the falsifiability criterion. The proposition P will be meaningful if some past person did verify or falsify P.

This position can be extended even farther. Let us suppose that there is an event E which occurred in the past and which was not observed by any person, nor was any person in a position to observe it. It might be claimed by the sceptic that statements about E are not verifiable or falsifiable. But we can say that such statements are meaningful if some person *could* have been *in a position* to verify or falsify them. If it is logically possible that *some* person *could* have been in a position to verify or falsify them, then this satisfies the requirement that they be verifiable or falsifiable *in principle*. And it seems that, given any past event, some person *could* have observed that past event. Hence propositions about past events are meaningful.

Do These Replies Succeed in Refuting the Verification Argument?

According to the third possible reply to the Verification Argument, a proposition P about the past is meaningful if and only if *some* person could have been in a position to verify or falsify P. Let us suppose that P is: "Event E had the property W." Then a person is in a position to verify or falsify P only if he is in a position to observe E. But to observe E, that person must be contemporaneous with E. He must observe E at the time E is occurring. But then the proposition the person is in a position to verify or falsify is not the proposition "Event E *had* the property W." For while the person *is* observing E he is in a position to verify or falsify a *present-tense* proposition about E rather than a past-tense proposition about E. But proposition P is a *past-tense* proposition about E. Therefore, the person who is observing E is not in a position to verify or falsify P. But then there is *no* position in which anyone could be such that he could verify or falsify P. Hence, P is meaningless. Therefore, all propositions about the past are meaningless, since this same argument could be given for each of them.

It follows from what has just been said that none of the three replies to the Verification Argument is satisfactory. Someone might have been in a position to verify or falsify a proposition in the present tense about *E*. But no one could ever be in a position to verify or falsify a past-tense proposition about *E*, for propositions about *E* can be verified or falsified only while *E* is occurring. Hence only *present-tense* propositions about *E* can be verified or falsified *because these are the only propositions that are about* E *while* E *is occurring. Observation of* E *can verify or falsify only those propositions that are about* E *while the observations are being made.* But only present-tense propositions about *E* are about *E* while the observations of *E* are being made. Hence only present-tense propositions about *E* can be verified or falsified by observing *E*. But observation of *E* is the only way in which a proposition about *E* can be conclusively verified or falsified. Hence no past-tense proposition about *E* can be verified or falsified. It follows from this that no past-tense proposition is meaningful. But all propositions purporting to express historical knowledge are in the past tense. Therefore no proposition purporting to express historical knowledge is meaningful.

This seems to show that all three replies given to the Verification Argument are unsatisfactory. For *P* is a past-tense proposition and yet each of those replies depended on someone's possibly *observing* the event *E*. In the first reply (pp. 145–146) it was said that the historian could have observed the Battle of Agincourt because it is logically possible that he might have existed at the time of that battle instead of existing now. But when the historian did observe the battle, he would have been verifying or falsifying a present-tense proposition. The second reply (pp. 146–149) claims that the Battle of Agincourt could have existed in the present so that the historian could have observed it in the present. But again, the historian would have been verifying or falsifying a present-tense proposition. The same is true of the third reply (pp. 149–150), since if someone other than the historian had been in a position to verify or falsify *P*, that person would have been contemporaneous with *E*—that is, that person would have observed E. But then that person could verify or falsify only present-tense propositions about E. But a present-tense and a past-tense proposition about E are different propositions. Hence, to verify or falsify one is not to verify or falsify the other. So none of the methods described in these three replies are possible methods of verifying or falsifying past-tense propositions, for they involve only the verification or falsification of present-tense propositions.

But a proponent of the three replies to the Verification Argument still might say that these replies in fact have not been shown to be unsatisfactory. He might say that past-tense propositions about E *can* be about E in the way required for them to be verifiable or falsifiable by observations of E. Let us again consider the two propositions:

(1) Event E has the property W.

(2) Event E had the property W.

These two propositions differ with respect to the tenses of their verbs, but, it might be said, in all other respects they are the same. These two propositions can be used to assert exactly the same thing about E. And, the proponent of the three replies will continue, this means that propositions (1) and (2) have exactly the same content. The tense of the verb only indicates when the propositions can be truly asserted: the present-tense proposition can be truly asserted only while E is occurring and the past-tense proposition can be truly asserted only after E has ceased to occur. So tenses have to do only with time of assertion of the proposition and not with *what is asserted* about E when the proposition is asserted. Difference in tense does not indicate difference in content.

How does this constitute a defense of the three replies against the objection to them raised at the beginning of this section? The objection was that observations of E could verify or falsify only present-tense propositions about E. But now the proponent of the three replies will claim that it is *what* is asserted about E, that is, *the content* of the present-tense proposition, which is verified or falsified by such observations. Such observations are relevant to the content only. Let us suppose that such observations verify the content of proposition (1). Then, the proponent will claim, those same observations verify the content of proposition (2) also, *since* (1) *and* (2) *have exactly the same content.* Therefore past-tense propositions can be verified or falsified by observations of past events while those events are occurring. It follows from this that the three replies to the Verification Argument are satisfactory.

I believe that the proponent of the second reply has not made an adequate defense of the three replies for the following reasons. Let us suppose that the proponent is correct in saying that propositions (1) and (2) have the same content. What is their content? How is this content to be expressed? The proponent would say that the content that (1) and (2) both have can be expressed by the following proposition:

(3) Event E has the property W.

But proposition (3) seems to be wholly identical with proposition (1). Yet proposition (3) is supposed to express only the content of proposition (1) and is not supposed to be identical with the whole of (1). Furthermore, how can proposition (3) express the content of proposition (2), for (3) seems to be a present-tense proposition and (2) is a past-tense proposition? Is the content of a past-tense proposition itself in the present tense? Moreover, if (3) is in the present tense, then (3) and (2) have a common content, which is expressible in proposition (4):

(4) Event E has the property W.

But then, since (4) is identical with (3), the same problems will arise about the relations between (4) and (2).

The proponent of the three replies would answer these difficulties by denying that proposition (3) was in the present tense. In fact, he would say that the verb in proposition (3), though it appears to be a present-tense verb, has no tense at all. The verb in proposition (3) is a "tenseless" verb. Propositions (1) and (2) each have two aspects, a content and a tense. By having no tense at all, proposition (3) represents only their content.

So it is clear that the three replies can be defended only if there are or can be tenseless verbs—only if there can be verbs which, as it is sometimes put, "make no reference to any particular time." I believe that it is doubtful that there are such verbs. Whether or not the Verification Argument is sound depends on whether or not the notion of a tenseless verb can be made coherent. If there can be no such verbs, the Verification Argument cannot be refuted in the ways suggested in this chapter.

CHAPTER NINE

𒐫𒐫𒐫𒐫𒐫𒐫𒐫𒐫

THE CONCEPT OF THE PAST

Introduction

Scepticism about historical knowledge can be based on arguments purporting to show that propositions about the past are meaningless. One such argument has been discussed in Chapter Eight. In this chapter I wish to discuss a quite different argument purporting to establish exactly the same conclusion: *that historical propositions are meaningless.* The sceptic may first assert that one can justifiably claim to have knowledge of some present state of affairs only if he understands the proposition that describes that state of affairs. At least this is true for propositions that describe states of affairs having a certain degree of complexity. For example, one can know that France and Germany are members of the Common Market only if one understands the proposition "France and Germany are members of the Common Market." It may be possible for one to know *that* this proposition is true without understanding the proposition. That is, it may be possible for one to have good reason to believe that this proposition is true—and we might be willing to call this "knowledge that this proposition is true"—even though one did not understand the proposition. But although one might know that the *proposition* is true in this way, one still could not claim to know the *fact* expressed or described by that proposition unless he understands that proposition. Understanding the proposition is a necessary (but not a sufficient) condition of knowing that fact. (And if only beings who have the use of language can be said to understand propositions, then only beings who have the use of language can be said to know facts of a certain degree of complexity.)

This applies to propositions about the past, too. One cannot be said to know that some state of affairs *was* the case unless one understands the proposition that expresses or describes that past fact. The sceptic then points out that propositions that express or describe past facts are in the past tense. And he claims that no one can understand propositions that express or describe past facts because no one can understand propositions (or sentences or statements) that are in the past tense. Such propositions are meaningless. Hence such propositions cannot express knowledge about the past.

This claim can also be put by saying that no one has or can have the concept of the past. That is, no one can understand *what it is* for an event *to be past*. Similarly, if a person is color-blind so that he has never observed red objects, he cannot know what it is for an object to be red; and this is expressed by saying that he does not have the concept of red. This is just the sort of claim that the sceptic is here making about the past, with two differences: the sceptic is saying that (1) *no one* (2) *can* have the concept of the past, not that *some* people *do not* have that concept. If the sceptic is right about this, it follows that there can be no such thing as knowledge of the past. For such knowledge presupposes the possession of the concept of the past. One must know what it is for some event or state of affairs to be past in order to be able to have knowledge of that event or state of affairs as being past. And since historical knowledge is knowledge of the past, it follows that there cannot be historical knowledge.

We certainly *seem* to have the concept of the past. We seem to know what it is for an event to be past rather than present or future. We talk about past events and apparently can communicate with others about such events. On what basis could the sceptic claim that we do not and cannot understand past-tense sentences (or statements or propositions) or understand what it is for an event to be past?

The sceptic would first point out that the fact that people talk in a certain way does not prove that they understand what they are purportedly talking about. An example from Leibniz may be used to support the sceptic here. People have probably talked about the fastest possible motion. Leibniz says: "At first glance, it might appear that we had the idea of the fastest motion, for we understand what we are saying. . . ."[1] But, Leibniz continues, we cannot have that idea or concept, which is to say that a person who ostensibly talks about the fastest motion does not in fact understand what he is saying. The reason why we cannot have the concept of the fastest motion is that, according to Leibniz, there can be no such thing as the fastest motion. It is not that in fact no motion that has taken place or is taking place is the fastest. Rather, no motion *can* be the fastest. Such a motion *can not* take place. Such a motion is not even possible. Since there can be no such thing, there is and can be nothing for the concept of "the fastest motion" to be the concept of. Every concept has and *must* have an object. Every concept is a concept *of* something, even if that something is only a possibility. Round squares are not possible, and no one can have the concept of a round square; no one can know what a round square would be or understand what would be meant by calling something a "round square." Similarly, if there can be nothing for the concept of the fastest motion to be the concept of, there can be no such concept. Leibniz argues that no motion can be the fastest in the following way: "Let us assume a wheel turning with the fastest motion; then it is easy to see that if one of the wheel's spokes were lengthened to extend beyond the rim, its end-point would be moving faster than a nail lying on the rim, whose motion is therefore not the fastest, which contradicts the hypothesis."[2] The assumption that a wheel is turning with the fastest motion leads to a contradiction; therefore that assumption is false. This proof is intended to show that there can be no such thing as the fastest motion. And if this proof does show this, then there can be no such thing as the concept of the fastest motion. People could believe that they do have this concept. They could appear to talk about the fastest motion. They could perhaps even try to invent a machine that could travel with the fastest motion. But if Leibniz has proved that there can be no such thing as "the fastest motion," then these people could not understand what could be meant by "the fastest motion." They could not have the concept of the fastest motion.

Thus, that we seem to understand past-tense sentences and that we seem to communicate with one another about the past does not prove that we understand these sentences or that we have the concept of the past. The sceptic asserts that in fact we do not understand these sentences and do not have this concept. More than this, he asserts that we *cannot* understand these sentences or have this concept. But he does not give the same *type* of argument for this sceptical thesis as that given by Leibniz with respect to "the fastest motion." If the sceptic were to give the same type of argument, he would try to show that the supposed concept of the past can have no object, just as Leibniz may have shown that the supposed concept of the fastest motion can have no object. That is, the sceptic would have to prove that there can be no such thing as a past event or a past state of affairs. And perhaps the sceptic could prove this. But the argument I will present in this chapter is not of that type.

Another type of argument the sceptic could give would be to show that some of our beliefs about past events form an inconsistent set of beliefs. However, the argument for the sceptic's position which we will consider in this chapter is of still another type. It purports to show that we do not have and cannot have the concept of the past because there is no way in which we could have acquired this concept. First the sceptic claims that if we could acquire the concept at all, we could do so only by either observation or by definition. We come to know what the term "red" means by observing red objects. This procedure is sometimes called "ostensive definition." Red objects are pointed out to the child and he is told that they are red. In this way he comes to have the concept of the color "red." He comes to know what the term "red" means and what it is for something to be red. We come to know what the term "circle" means by a different type of definition, namely a discursive definition. We never observe a circle— a plane geometric figure every point on whose circumference is a certain fixed distance from a point within the figure. We sometimes observe figures that approach this ideal; but as they never do fit this definition perfectly, we cannot obtain the concept of a circle in the same way as the concept of the color "red." We obtain it by what is sometimes called a genus-species definition.

But neither of these methods is available in the case of the concept of the past. Ostensive definition is not available, for we never observe the past or a past event—every event we can observe is a present event. And there is no genus-species definition of "the past" or "a past event." Thus, the sceptic would continue, there is no way in which we could have acquired the concept of the past. Hence we do not and cannot have the concept of the past. That is, we cannot understand sentences (or statements or propositions) about the past. (We may *seem* to understand such sentences; but this does not prove that we *do* understand them, as the example from Leibniz may show.) It follows from this that we cannot have historical knowledge.

In the sections to follow I will discuss certain replies to this argument for historical scepticism. Each of these replies purports to describe a method by which we can acquire the concept of the past. I will show that none of these replies is satisfactory.

Memory and Ostensive Definition of "Past Event"

It will be objected at this point that the possibility of ostensive definition was ruled out too hastily. In fact, we do apprehend past events, not through the senses as we apprehend the color "red," but through memory. We are "directly in touch with" past events through memory, just as we are "directly in touch with" present events through the senses. Thus we can obtain the concept of the past by "observation" (through memory) of past events. In this way an ostensive definition of the expression "past event" can be given.

The sceptic can reply that if this method of obtaining the concept of the past by ostensive definition is to work, we must know *that* certain of our experiences are memory experiences. Otherwise, we will not know which experiences to use in our ostensive definition of the expression "past event." But to know that an experience is a memory experience is to know that it is related in some way to a past event. Thus we must already know what the expression "past event" means—we must already have the concept of a past event—in order to know what the expression "memory experience" means or to know what memory experiences are, so as to identify experiences as *memory* experiences, and hence to use this method of ostensive definition. But if we already have the concept of a past event, we do not need to use this method. And if we do not have this concept, we cannot use this method. But we either do or do not already have this concept. Hence, use of this method would be either superfluous or impossible.

A procedure which does not involve the use of memory is as follows: One might define "past event" in terms of "present event" and the relation of "before and after." "Present event" might be defined as "event that can be observed now by the use of the senses." Then "past event" would be defined as "event that is before a present event." The difficulty with this is that a person must know what the term "now" means in order to understand this definition. But the meaning of "now" is closely connected with the concepts of past and future. It is doubtful whether someone who does not already know what it is for an event to be past can know what it is for an observation to be taking place "now." That is, it seems that a person must already have the concept of the past in order to understand this definition. But couldn't "present event" be defined ostensively instead? Even if this could be done, it is still the case that the sense of "before" used in the definition of "past event" is that of "temporally before." And how can a person acquire the concept of *temporal* priority if he does not already have the concept of the past? This question will be discussed further in a later section (pp. 171–172).

The Use of the Past Tense

One way of showing how we acquire the concept of the past, and thus of refuting this type of sceptical argument, is to show how we learn or can learn the use of the past tense. To have a given concept may be to have the ability to use the expressions and other linguistic forms associated with that concept. For example, having the concept of the color "red" may be identical with having the ability to use the term "red" or some synonym properly. What else could it mean to say of someone that he had the concept of "red"? And if to have a concept is to have a certain linguistic ability, then since actual uses of certain linguistic expressions will be good evidence that the person possesses that linguistic ability, so such actual uses will also be good evidence that the person possesses the corresponding concept.

Actual uses of such expressions may not be conclusive proof of the possession of a linguistic ability. The person in question may have used the term "red" in several situations in which red objects were present. But this finite number of uses might not prove beyond doubt that he has the concept of red, because later he may start using the term "red" in the presence of blue objects. For example, the person may, up to that time, have used it only with red objects because he had seen only red objects and had believed that the term "red" meant what *we* mean by "is either red or blue." If the person does start using the term "red" with blue objects, we have a choice between saying (1) that he did not have the linguistic ability to use "red" properly in the first place, even though he happened to use "red" properly (only with red objects); or (2) that he formerly had the ability to use "red" correctly, but does not now have that ability (since he is now using the term with blue objects). Since the first of these alternatives is always available in principle, we cannot take a finite number of correct uses of an expression as proof that the person has the linguistic ability in question. However, such correct uses constitute very good evidence that he has that ability. Hence, if it appears that a person learns to use the linguistic expression correctly, this will be good evidence that he has acquired the requisite ability. And since the ability is assumed to be identical with the concept, showing that he can learn to use the expression or linguistic form correctly will prove that he can acquire the concept in question.

This seems to be what lies behind attempts to show that we can acquire the concept of the past by showing that we can learn to use the past tense. The past tense is the linguistic form associated with the concept of the past, just as the expression "red" is associated with the concept of the color "red." We will examine what is probably the best attempt of this type, that of Edward J. Bond.[3]

Bond first describes an example of a child being taught the use of the past tense. The child is taught to say "is green" when a green light is showing and to say "was green" when a green light was previously but is not now showing. Even if this is not how people learn to use the past tense, surely they *could* learn to use it in this way. And the *possibility* of learning to use it in this way is all that is required to refute the sceptic, for that this is possible entails that it is possible to acquire the concept of the past.

But it will be objected that this method employs memory since the child has to remember that the light was green in order to be justified in *now* saying "was green." Bond admits that memory is involved in this way: ". . . the only way in which we can learn the use of the past tense is in circumstances similar to this, circumstances, in other words, in which we can say that it was learned by remembering."[4] But if memory is employed, isn't it presupposed that the child already has the concept of the past (for the reasons given earlier (p. 160) in this chapter)? Bond continues:

If this is true, it follows that it is only in such circumstances, when the event in question is in the very recent past, and so remembered by any normal person who has his attention fixed on the phenomenon in question, that we can say that it is necessarily true that something was the case or occurred or happened, on the grounds that this is what is meant by so saying.[5]

Bond's argument here seems to be this: The child learning the use of the past tense can use memory because *he* does not have to determine which of his experiences are memory experiences and which are not. That is, *he* does not have to decide which of his experiences give him knowledge of the past and which do not; and therefore *he* does not already have to have the concept of the past. But *we* (the observer of the child) do have to have the concept of the past already because we have to identify certain of *our* experiences as memory experiences. Only if the child correctly uses the past tense can *we* justifiably say that he has acquired the concept of the past. Therefore, we have to be able to determine in which cases the child has correctly said "was green" and in which cases (if any) he has not correctly said it. And to determine this, we must determine when the green light had in fact been on and when it had not been on, since the child *correctly* says "was green" only when the green light had been on. But are *we* certain that the green light had been on on those occasions when the child says "was green"? We remember that it was on, but can *we* be sure that our memories of this are correct? Bond's answer, as given in the passage quoted above, is that when the event in question occurred in the very recent past, "any normal person who has had his attention fixed on the phenomenon in question" must have remembered it. Clearly Bond is saying that memory beliefs about very recent past events are such that we would not accept evidence against these beliefs. (See Chapter Seven, pp. 135–139, for a discussion of another view of this sort.)

Let us assume that Bond's reply concerning the use of memory is sound. And let us also suppose that the child can learn to use the past tense correctly with respect to events in the very recent past. Does this show that he has the concept of the past? If he can use the past tense correctly *only* with respect to the very recent past, we certainly could not say that he had the concept of the past. In order to be said to have that concept, he must also be able to use the past tense in making statements about less recent events. The past contains both recent and not-so-recent events. The child must be able to speak correctly about both types of events if he has the concept of the past. But if he learns to speak correctly about very recent past events, does he then also know how to speak correctly about less recent events?

Bond claims that he can also then speak correctly about less recent events. He says: "And once we have mastered the use of the past tense in any one sort of case, we do not need to master a new technique for every new sort of case, since the use of the past tense has the same signification in all cases."[6] Bond is certainly right in saying that the past tense, as we *do in fact* use it, has the same import in all of its uses, that is, with respect to recent and to not-so-recent events. But the question is, has the child learned by this procedure how to use the past tense *as we do in fact use it*? Or has he learned to use it only partly as we use it, that is, only with respect to very recent events? Bond *claims* that the child has learned to use the past tense with respect to events at any point in the past. But he does not *prove* that the child has done so. The use of the past tense may have the same import in all cases, but has the child learned, by this procedure of dealing only with very recent events, that the use of the past tense has the same import in *all* cases? What, in fact, has the child learned by this procedure?

The child may have learned that the past tense is to be used *only* with respect to very recent past events. After all, he has been taught to use it only with such events. Second, he may have come to believe that one can use the past tense *only when* one is absolutely certain that the event has occurred, that is, only when one is relying on a memory belief against which one will not accept evidence. In fact, it would seem that the child would have to believe these two things about the use of the past tense. An analogy may be drawn at this point to the following example of ostensive definition (of which Bond's procedure is another example). Smith is ostensively defining "automobile" for Jones; but every automobile that Smith points out to Jones is blue; if Jones has learned his lesson correctly, he must now believe that the word Smith is trying to teach him means "blue conveyance with wheels, etc." Jones must now believe that "having a blue color" is part of the meaning of "automobile." The doctrine of ostensive definition is partly that every property which the examples (in this case, automobiles) have in common is to be taken as part of the meaning of the term being ostensively defined. This case is analogous to the case of the child and the past tense because the child is being taught to use the past tense by an ostensive procedure. Cases in which certain events are in the very recent past are presented to him and he is taught to associate the use of the past tense with cases similar to these, just as Jones was taught to associate "automobile" with certain types of objects. The past events here have a precisely parallel role in this procedure to the role of the automobiles in the analogous case of Smith and

Jones. Since an ostensive procedure is being used, the child must associate *all* of the characteristics those cases have in common with the use of the past tense, just as Jones must associate all of the properties (for example, blue) the automobiles have in common with the meaning of the term "automobile." The child could not justifiably do anything else. He could not justifiably pick out only certain characteristics of those cases to associate with the use of the past tense, for he would have no reason to pick out *those* common characteristics and not include others also. Yet if he did include all of the features common to all of the cases presented to him, he would have to conclude that the past tense was to be used only with respect to very recent events and to events against his memory beliefs about which he would not accept evidence, just as Jones would have to conclude that the term "automobile" could be correctly applied only if the object in question was blue.

But not all past events are events of these types, that is, events that are very recent or events against his memory beliefs about which he would not accept evidence. The child would not have learned to use the past tense with respect to events that are not of these types. Hence he would not have *our* concept of the past. It may be replied that the child has *a* concept of the past. But that the child can acquire the concept he does acquire will not refute scepticism about historical knowledge. For statements of historians that are couched in the past tense are typically about events that are neither very recent nor of which we have memory beliefs we regard as certain. Thus, in order to understand most, if not all, propositions about historical events, the child would have to acquire *our* concept of the past. Furthermore, no ostensive or quasi-ostensive procedure could be used to teach the child our concept of the past because (less-than-recent) historical events cannot be brought back from the past to be used as examples in ostensive procedures. Nor, in general, is anyone now living who remembers these events in the way required by Bond's ostensive procedure (for example, one who was a participant in the event in question).

Perhaps, however, there is some other way to teach the child to extend his use of the past tense to less recent events and to events about which one does not have absolutely certain memory beliefs. Bond suggests this in discussing criteria and evidence. Apparently he feels that the ostensive process teaches the child that a past event is one of which the following conditional is true: If someone *had been* in the proper circumstances, that person *could have* observed that event (just as the child himself did observe the green light). The child is supposed to learn that "ϕ was the case" *means* "if someone had been in the proper position, he could have observed such-and-such." And the child is supposed to learn that this is what "ϕ was the case" means for *any* ϕ, whether ϕ is the description of a recent event or a less recent event. But, as we have seen, he has in fact learned what "ϕ was the case" means only with respect to very recent events that he is absolutely certain have occurred.

How can the child be taught what "ϕ was the case" means when ϕ is a description of a less recent event? One method might be this: We can tell him that where ϕ is the description of a different sort of event (for example, a less recent event), then "ϕ was the case" means "if someone had been in the proper position at the proper time, he could have observed such-and-such." But could this method in fact be used? It could be used only if the child were able to understand this conditional which allegedly expresses the meaning of "ϕ was the case." This conditional concerns possible events—namely, possible observations—that might have or could have taken place in the *past*. Therefore this conditional is itself about the past. Furthermore, this conditional is about less recent past events, namely, the possible observations. Therefore this conditional cannot be used in teaching the child to understand past-tense expressions about less recent events, for use of this conditional presupposes that the child can *already* understand this conditional and thus that the child *already* understands expressions about less recent past events (namely, the possible observations). But how did the child learn what conditionals about less recent events mean? The meaning of these conditionals cannot be taught to him ostensively, for we cannot *now* put someone in the proper position to observe a past event. In fact, it is implausible to suppose that the child could learn the meaning of conditionals about less recent past events until he had learned the meaning of simple declarative sentences about less recent past events, for surely it would be much easier to teach him the latter than the former. It may even be true that one *must* learn the meaning of declaratives before one can learn the meaning of conditionals, depending on how one regards the relation between conditionals and declaratives. Consequently, it seems doubtful that the child could be taught by a quasi-ostensive process to learn to use the past tense in the way in which we use it. Hence, it seems doubtful that the child can acquire the concept of the past in this way.

Observing Past Events

The sceptic claims that the concept of the past cannot be acquired by either ostensive or genus-species definitions. We have just considered a theory that does attempt to use an ostensive procedure for acquiring this concept. This theory was found to be inadequate. Now we turn to a position that attempts to employ a different ostensive procedure for the same purpose. This procedure is based on the doctrine of the "specious present." It is alleged that past events *can* be directly observed through use of the senses because some past events exist in the "specious present."

The expression "the specious present" refers to the

putative fact that the present we are aware of or experience is not an instant. We are not aware of instants; we are aware of intervals, even though these intervals may be very small. A. D. Woozley employs this putative fact in the following way. First he states that we do obtain the concept of a past event by observing past events *as past* or *when they are past*. Thus, this procedure is just as much an ostensive procedure as the procedure whereby one acquires the concept of the color "red" by observing red objects. "The fact is that a man can acquire the notion of pastness in precisely the same way as he acquires the notion of red, *viz.* empirically, by seeing an instance of it."[7] Then Woozley uses the notion of the specious present to explain how we can *see* "instances of pastness." "The present is not for our awareness an instantaneous click of a camera shutter with no perceptible duration. It has a perceptible duration, within which we are aware that one stage precedes another, in other words, within which we are aware of an instance of pastness."[8] The example Woozley gives is that of motion. We are aware *in the present* of a cat walking from left to right. Hence we must be aware, still in the present, of the cat being at the left and starting to move from left to right. But why is the cat's starting to move from left to right to be regarded as a past event? Woozley's argument for this is: "To say that something is past is to say that it occurred before something else; and we are aware of one thing happening before another whenever, for instance we see any movement, such as a cat walking across the floor."[9] We see the cat's reaching a position further to the right. And we are aware in the present that the event of the cat's starting at the left is *before* the event of the cat's reaching a position further to the right. Hence, in the present we are aware of a past event, namely the cat's starting from the left. Hence, we can acquire the concept of the past by an ostensive procedure.[10]

This theory is untenable. The event of the cat's starting

to move from the left is a past event because it occurs before another event. But this event of the cat's starting to move from the left is also a present event because we are aware of it in the specious present. That is, we are aware of two events in the same specious present; but one is temporally before the other and hence is called "past." Thus, one and the same event can be both present and past. But the terms "past" and "present" are usually used so that no event can be both past and present. Hence it is doubtful whether *our* concept of the past can be acquired in the way indicated by Woozley, since he may not be using the terms "past" and "present" in the way we do.

But, more important, this method also seems to be subject to the same difficulty involved in the view that we acquire the concept of the past by learning how to use the past tense. Woozley apparently supposes that we learn what it is for an event to be past solely from observing very recent past events, namely, those events that are past but are also within the specious present. He probably supposes this because according to his definition of "past event" an event is past if it occurred before some other event. And if past events were observed in the present, as he claims, it might seem that the only characteristic *these* past events have that distinguishes them from the present events also observed in the present is that these past events are before these present events. But this is not true. *These* past events all have at least one other characteristic in common, namely, they are very recent. Therefore, what the person will learn by *observing* these and only these past events—that is, only past events which at the time of being observed are within the specious present—is that "past event" means "an event that has very recently occurred before some other event." But this would not be *our* concept of a past event, for we believe there can be and are past events that are not recent. Yet only very recent past events can be observed according to Woozley's method. Hence, this method cannot enable us to acquire *our* concept of a past event.

Observing Temporal Priority

There is another possible position concerning the acquisition of the concept of a past event. It is this: Instead of the expression "past event" being ostensively defined, what is ostensively defined is the expression "temporally prior to." We experience in the specious present two events, one of which is temporally prior to the other. That is, we experience an instance of the relation "temporally prior to." Hence this expression "temporally prior to" is *ostensively* defined. Then we give a discursive definition of "past event" which makes use of this ostensive definition of "temporally prior to": "Past event" means "an event that is temporally prior to a present event." So we need not say that either event which is experienced in the specious present is a past event because we do not need an instance of a past event in order to define "past event." We can say that both events in the specious present are present events. And we thus answer the objection that this type of theory must say of certain events that they are both past and present. On the view stated above, all events experienced in the specious present are present events. A discursive definition is then given of the expression "past event."

But this procedure for acquiring the concept of the past is subject to a serious difficulty. It is alleged that we learn the meaning of "temporally prior to" by an ostensive procedure, that is, experiencing instances of this relation. But if the meaning of this expression is learned by a wholly ostensive procedure, every property common to those observed instances of this relation must be taken as part of the meaning of this expression. One property that is common to those instances is the property "holds between present events." That is, every instance of this relation we experience is an instance holding between present events. But most, and perhaps all, events that *we* regard as past are not also present events. Since they are not also present events, they cannot stand in the relation of temporal priority to some other events since, by the above ostensive definition of "temporally prior to," only present events can stand in that relation. Consequently, very few or none of the events *we* regard as past events would turn out to be past events on this procedure. Hence this procedure cannot be used for acquiring the concept of the past.

Scepticism and the Concept of the Past

We have now examined four different theories concerning the question of how we acquire the concept of the past. Each of these theories has, I believe, been shown to be inadequate. If no theory about this question is adequate, then either we do not have to acquire the concept of the past or else we do not have the concept of the past but only appear to have it. It is possible to maintain that we do not have to acquire the concept of the past on the grounds that everyone already has that concept. The concept is not derived from experience, as is the concept of a chair, but instead is *a priori*; that is, the concept is had merely in virtue of one's being a human being. But theories asserting that certain concepts are *a priori* involve many difficulties.

If we do not and cannot have the concept of the past, but only appear to have it, then by the argument given at the beginning of this chapter (pp. 155–156), we do not and cannot understand propositions about the past. And if we do not and cannot understand such propositions, then we do not and cannot have historical knowledge about the past.

CHAPTER TEN

𝕮𝕮𝕮𝕮𝕮𝕮𝕮𝕮𝕮𝕮

CAN THE PAST CHANGE?

Introduction

Many people believe that the past cannot change. That is, no change can occur in a past event while it is past. They believe not only that changes *do not* occur in the past but also that they *cannot* occur in the past. Changes can occur only in the present. In this chapter I will examine that belief.

The first section introduces the notion of change in the past and contains another objection to the theories of how we acquire the concept of the past; this objection involves the notion of change in the past. In the next section it is shown how the possibility of changes in the past leads to scepticism about historical knowledge. The final section contains a defense of the possibility of such changes against an attempt by Miss G. E. M. Anscombe to show that they are not possible.

The Concept of the Past and the Concept of a Past Event

In the previous chapter we considered theories about how the concept of the past can be acquired. But exactly what concept is it that these theories are supposed to show how we can acquire? At various points in Chapter Nine the expressions "the concept of the past," "the concept of a past event," and "the concept of pastness" were used. Do all of these expressions denote the same concept? If not, how does the concept denoted by one of these expressions differ from the concepts denoted by the others? And which of these concepts is it necessary that persons be able to acquire if they are to be able to have historical knowledge?

The first two expressions, at least, denote different concepts. The concept of the past is different from the concept of a past event. We think of "the past" as a realm in which reside events that have already occurred. We talk of events being "in the past" and of being inaccessible to present observation because they are "in the past." And many people view the historian as probing or investigating this realm called "the past." It is also believed by many that events that have occurred continue to exist in the past—to be past is to have a certain mode of existence. The following passage from C. D. Broad illustrates this position:

It might be said that, when an event is past, it ceases to exist. . . . This objection seems to me to be mistaken. It depends on a view of time and change which I am forced to reject. It appears to me that, once an event has happened, it exists eternally; all that happens henceforth to it is that, as more and more events occur and take their permanent place in the ever-lengthening temporal order of the universe, it retreats into the more and more distant past. If an event ceased to exist as soon as it ceased to be present it plainly could no longer stand in any relation to anything. But, when we say that it is past, we imply that it does stand in the relation of temporal precedence to the present; moreover we say that one past event precedes a second past event and follows a third. All such statements would be nonsense if events ceased to exist when they ceased to be present.[1]

We will assume that past events do exist in the past in the way described by Broad.

Thus there are relations between the concept of the past and the concept of a past event: the past "contains" or is made up of past events. Yet the two concepts are different, since the past is different from past events as a class differs from its members. But the past is not just a class of past events; rather, it is an *ordered* class of past events. Past events stand in relations of "before and after" to one another; past events are believed to maintain these relations to one another while they are in the past.

We can show in another way that these two concepts are different. First, many believe that past events do not change after they occur. If Napoleon issued a certain order at a certain moment in the campaign in Russia, it is still the case now that Napoleon rather than one of his generals issued that order. Events become "fixed" as soon as they occur. Changes in events do not occur while those events are past. Second, as has been noted, events stand in certain relations of "before and after" to one another while they are in the past. And it is believed that these relations, as well as the events themselves, do not change. If the Franco-Prussian War occurred after the Thirty Years' War, then the first event is still after the second event when both are past. Third, it is believed that no events occur (or can occur) in the past. Every event in the past has been present at some time or other. No event can be past without having been present.

In the preceding paragraph we have spoken of events as now being this or that way in the past. Can we talk about events *now* being a certain way in the past? Are sentences of this sort meaningful at all? What can such sentences mean? It is as if such sentences referred to two time scales, one showing that the event is past and the other showing that the event is now a certain way. The question of the meaningfulness of such sentences is discussed in the following sections. In this section we will assume that such sentences about possible changes in the past are meaningful.

The first type of change just mentioned is a change in individual events, as well as a change in the past itself. But the second type of change is a change in certain relations between and among events and is not a change in the events themselves. But if this second type of change did occur, it would be a change in the past, though not a change in the past events involved. It would be a change in the past because we are regarding the past as an ordered class, the ordering relation between past events being that of before and after. Suppose we have an ordered class containing just two members, Abraham and Isaac, in that order. The members of this ordered couple are ordered by the relation "father of" since Abraham was the father of Isaac. This class is different from the ordered couple consisting of Isaac and Abraham in *that* order, as can be seen from the fact that the ordering relation in this second ordered couple is a different relation, namely "son of" instead of "father of." Although two nonordered classes are regarded as identical if and only if they have exactly the same members, *ordered* classes are regarded as identical if and only if they have the same members *ordered in the same way*. Thus two ordered couples are identical if and only if the first member of one is identical with the first member of the other and the second member of one is identical with the second member of the other.

Suppose, then, there was a change such that past event *x* is now *after* past event *y* instead of before *y* as it previously was. This would entail that the past is now different, because the past is an *ordered* class and there has been a change in the order of its members. But although the past has changed, there has not necessarily been a change in past events *x* and *y*. Hence the past is distinct from past events. That there is a change in the former does not entail that there is a change in the latter. Hence the concept of the past is distinct from the concept of a past event. This is also shown by the third type of change mentioned above. The third type of change consists in an event's occurring in the past rather than in the present. An event would thus be added to the past. And the past would have changed, because a class becomes a different class when it has different members from those it previously had, though no event already past would have changed. (In a sense, the past is constantly changing; events are being added to the past at the point at which the past borders on the present, since present events are continually becoming past. But this is not the sort of change we are concerned with in this chapter.)

Having shown that the concept of the past is different

from the concept of a past event, we can now see that the three methods discussed in Chapter Nine can *at most* show how we can acquire the concept of *a past event*, not the concept of *the past*. These methods involve the observing and experiencing of individual *events*. Thus we can, at most, learn about individual *events* in these ways. We cannot learn in these ways that *the past* is an "unchanging realm" in which events reside. So even if these methods were sound, they could be used only to acquire the concept of a past event. And we have seen that they are not sound even for that purpose.

Scepticism and Changes in the Past

Several types of changes in the past—changes in past events and the past itself—have been described in the preceding section. That these changes can be described gives rise to another sceptical argument about the possibility of historical knowledge.

Historical knowledge or knowledge of past events is usually taken to be knowledge of events as they were when those events occurred and knowledge of events as they now are in the past. But the sceptic might say: At most the historian can have knowledge only of events as they occurred. One remembers events as they were when they occurred, not as they are now in the past. Yet since these events can change in the past, these events might be different now as past events from the way they were when they were occurring as present events. And the past itself might be different from the way it is taken to be on the basis of the occurrence of these events and the order in which they occurred. Changes are possible in past events and in the past itself; that such changes are possible is shown by the fact that they can be given noncontradictory descriptions such as those given in the previous section. But there is no way of finding out about changes that occur in the past or in past events. Neither memory nor evidence can be used for this purpose, because memory and evidence relate to events only as those events were when they occurred, not as they now are. Hence the historian cannot find out about the past and past events as they now are. But historical propositions seem to be about both events as they occurred *and* as they now are. When a historian says: "Danton ordered the arrest of several aristocrats," he means this both as a description of what happened when it happened and as it now is in the past. But since the past and past events may have changed in the past and therefore may now be different from what they were when they occurred, this statement and other historical statements may be false. Hence, the sceptic concludes, the historian cannot *know* that any given historical proposition is true. That is to say, historical knowledge is not possible.

It might be replied that this is a very limited kind of scepticism, since to eliminate this scepticism, all we need to do is to confine the reference of historical propositions to events as they were when they occurred. That is, we need only specify that such propositions are to be taken as describing past events as they were at the time of their occurrence and not as they now are. Thus, if the past did change, such changes could not render these propositions false, because these propositions are not about past events as they *are* but rather about past events as they *were* before any possible changes in them could have taken place. Hence if these propositions are true, they will remain true regardless of changes in the past of the kinds described above.

I believe that this reply to the sceptic is untenable and that this scepticism is of a far more serious kind than this reply indicates. The main reason for supposing that there is now a past—that is, for supposing (as C. D. Broad and many others do) that past events continue to exist after they occur and now exist *as past*—is that only if they do *now* exist (as past) *can* historical propositions (among others) be true. It is usually believed that historical propositions are true if and only if they correspond to past events. And when a historical proposition is *now* expressed, that proposition is *now* true if and only if that proposition *now* corresponds to the event in question. But in order for that proposition to correspond now to that event, that event must *now* exist. And the proposition must be true of that event as that event *now* is, since this is what is meant by the proposition and the event *now* corresponding. Therefore, historical propositions are about past events as they *now* are or as they are when those propositions are expressed, not exclusively about past events as they were when they occurred. Hence changes in past events after the occurrence of those events can render historical propositions false. And since we cannot know whether or not such changes have occurred, we cannot know whether or not historical propositions are true. Therefore, historical knowledge is not possible.

One wants to reply here that past-tense propositions do not now correspond to events as they now are, but rather to events as they were when they occurred. To support this reply, however, one would have to show how a relation, such as "corresponding to," can *now* exist between two entities (a proposition and an event) when only *one* of those entities (the proposition) *now* exists. We do, of course, assert relational propositions about two things, only one of which now exists. For example, we say sometimes, "That chair is just like the one we used to own," thus asserting a relation of similarity between a presently existing chair and one that no longer exists. But what does this assertion of similarity mean? Does it mean that the present chair has one or more properties the past chair also had? And if this is what the assertion means, can something of this sort be said about the proposition and the past event? Or does the assertion of similarity mean that if the past chair *were* present, it *would* present the same appearance as the present chair (thus bringing in all of the problems associated with counterfactual conditionals)? If the view is denied that true past-tense propositions are those that correspond with events now existing as past, then some other theory of truth for past-tense propositions must be presented.

But an even more powerful reply to the sceptic seems possible. Three types of changes in the past have been described in the previous section. As was noted in that section, there seems to be something unreal about these descriptions, as if they were descriptions of the impossible or as if the descriptions themselves were meaningless. What can it mean to say that a past event can change *in the past?* What could possibly be conveyed by these words? If one could show that these descriptions were meaningless, one could then assert that the changes they purport to describe are impossible, that such changes *cannot* occur. After all, the statement "This square is round" is meaningless; and there cannot be any round squares. If one could show that putative descriptions of changes in the past are meaningless, one would have shown that there *cannot* be any changes in past events after they occur. And the form of scepticism under consideration will have been refuted, since that form depends on the possibility of such changes.

The descriptions of changes in the past given in the previous section are not themselves contradictory. They are not of the form "*p* and not-*p*." But we have already seen in connection with the expression "the fastest motion" that a noncontradictory description may be a description of something that is impossible. However, one cannot merely say to the sceptic that the past cannot change, that such changes are impossible. Since he can give noncontradictory descriptions of such changes and hence has grounds for saying that such changes are possible, in order to refute him one would have to *prove* that the past cannot change. One must prove that the past not only *does not* change but also *could not* change.

When Does a Given Change in the Past Occur?

G. E. M. Anscombe has discussed the question: Why can't the past change? She regards this as a problem for a reason quite different from that of the possibility of scepticism about historical knowledge. Rather, she considers the question of the possibility of having present criteria for historical propositions. If present evidence provided criteria for statements about the past, that is, if such evidence *conclusively* determined the truth or falsity of such statements, then changes in the present could bring about changes in the past. But, Miss Anscombe claims, changes in the past are impossible. Hence changes in the past cannot be caused by changes in the present.

Miss Anscombe goes on to consider why the second premise, "changes in the past are impossible," is true. First, she tries to prove that the statement "the past can change" is not false, but meaningless. Presumably, showing that an apparently meaningful statement is meaningless is one way of showing that what the statement apparently asserts cannot exist or take place. Her argument is this:

> But "a change in the past" is *nonsense*, as can be seen from the fact that if a change occurs we can ask for its date. If the idea of a change in the past made sense, we could ask the question "When was the battle of Hastings in 1066?" . . . This could of course be given a sense in a particular context—say of a change in a system of dating. But until one gives it sense in some such way—which does not serve one's purpose—it is nonsensical. This consideration helps to remove the impression that when one says "the past cannot change" one is saying of something *intelligible* that it is an impossibility.[2]

What Miss Anscombe may be saying here is this: Every change can be dated. Moreover, it is *necessarily* the case that every change can be dated. It is part of the concept of a change that changes must be datable. Changes do, and must, take place at definite times and hence can be dated. Similarly, it is part of the concept of a circle that circles have centers. And just as it can always meaningfully be asked of a circle "Where is its center?" so it can always meaningfully be asked of a change when it occurred. And, just as importantly, these questions must be answerable. If the question about circles has no answer—if an answer is in principle impossible—then the object in question is not and cannot be a circle. And if the question about changes cannot in principle be answered, then what is being talked about is not and cannot be a change. But the question "When did it take place?" cannot be answered for changes in the battle of Hastings or in any other past event. If there were an answer to such a question, it would take the form "The battle of Hastings of 1066 changed in 1242." But such an answer cannot be given to this question, for such an answer itself seems to be meaningless. What could it mean to say "The battle of Hastings of 1066 changed in 1242"? Since such an answer is meaningless and since no other answer seems possible, there is no possible answer to the question "When did the change in the battle of Hastings take place?" There is no possible answer to such questions about any alleged change in the past. Hence it is not meaningful to talk about "changes in the past." Hence such changes are impossible. And the demonstration of this impossibility refutes the sceptic in the way indicated at the end of the previous section (p. 180).

But is it in principle impossible to date changes in past events and in the past itself? We might view the matter in the following way: Suppose a change occurs in the battle of Hastings after that battle is over. For example, suppose that Harold took part in the battle when it occurred, but after the change in that past battle he was no longer a participant in that battle. At some point in time Harold ceased to take (or to have taken) part in the battle of Hastings. This means that up to a certain point in time, say up to July 20, 1955, the proposition "Harold participated in the battle of Hastings" is true and after that date that proposition is false. In this way we can date the change in the past battle of Hastings: the change occurred on July 20, 1955. We can date changes in past events by dating changes in the truth values of propositions about those past events. If the possibility of changes in the past depends solely on being able to assign dates to such changes, then such changes are possible. Thus the question "When did the change in that past event take place?" can in principle be answered. Hence Miss Anscombe's argument does not show that changes in the past are impossible.

Miss Anscombe might reply that even this possibility of dating changes in the past would not render statements about changes in the past meaningful. She says that statements about changes in the past have no use. ". . . To speak of a change in the past is to produce an expression for which no use exists and which therefore has *no* sense."[3] One reply that could be made to the above suggested method of dating changes in past events is as follows: This method does not show that changes in past events can, even in principle, be dated, because this method is not a method that can in principle be used; we could never find out that the truth value of a proposition about a past event had changed; so we would never be able to assign dates to alleged changes in past events. This may also be what Miss Anscombe means when she says that expressions about changes in past events have no use. She may mean that no conditions or situations arise or exist in which we would talk about changes in past events. An expression is meaningful if and only if there are situations in which that expression could be used. These are no situations in which we would talk about round squares. Hence the expression "round square" is meaningless. (That round squares would have contradictory properties is the reason why there are no situations in which we would talk about them.) Miss Anscombe is claiming that there are no situations in which we would talk about changes in past events. She would probably also claim that there are no situations in which we would talk about changes in the truth values of past-tense propositions. Hence she would say that the expressions "a change in the past" and "a change in the truth value of a past-tense proposition" are both meaningless. And since the latter expression is meaningless, it cannot be used to give meaning to the former expression. To say that there are no situations in which we would use these expressions is to say that no evidence would be found such that we would speak of a change in past events or a change in the truth value of past-tense propositions on the basis of such evidence.

That an expression does not have a use shows that the expression does not have a meaning. And in this sense it shows that the expression is meaningless. But Miss Anscombe wants to say more than this. She wants to say that the expression "a change in the past" *could not* have a use, not that it merely does not happen to have a use.[4] She wants to say that this expression is meaningless in this much stronger sense of "meaningless." And it is this stronger position that one who is trying to refute the sceptic would want to maintain also. Statements about alleged changes in the past seemingly could not possibly have any meaning.

Only this stronger position would refute the sceptic. The sceptic would be willing to admit that expressions about changes in the past now have no use. But he would say that they could be given uses. Conditions could perhaps be specified in which we would or could speak about changes in the past. Hence there would be some reason to say that statements about changes in the past are or could be meaningful.

Miss Anscombe does not attempt to prove that such expressions could not be given uses. And it might seem that the sceptic is right. Why couldn't we specify certain situations in which we could talk about changes in the past?

I believe that such situations could be specified and, hence, that statements about changes in the past could be regarded as meaningful. First, we must distinguish between (1) specifying such situations in some conceptual scheme, and (2) specifying such situations in the conceptual scheme we now employ.

To take (1) first, it would be possible to specify such situations if we regarded the "remains of the past" in a different way from the way in which we now regard them. If we regarded present "remains" or evidence as criteria of the truth or falsity of statements about the past in the way previously explained, rather than as evidence about the past, then, as Miss Anscombe has pointed out, a change in the present "remains" will indicate a change in the past.

But perhaps an expression should not be regarded as possibly meaningful unless it can be given a use in the conceptual system we now use. The use just specified might be said to involve a change in our conceptual system. It involves treating "remains" as criteria, whereas we now treat them as evidence. Let us assume that this does involve a change in our conceptual system. Can we specify a situation in which we could talk about a change in the past without such a change in our conceptual system?

Let us assume that a person believes in the existence of God and believes that God communicates with man on occasion. And let us assume that a Roman ruin suddenly disappears one day but that no cause for its disappearance can be found. The disappearance of this ruin might be taken by this person as a sign by God that the past has changed in such a way that the building (of which the ruin is the remains) no longer plays the role in past events it once played. And in general, in cases of changes in "remains" for which no present causes can be found, those changes are taken by this person as signs from God concerning changes in the past. It is very likely that this person would not be justified in taking these changes as signs in this way, but his so taking them is a meaningful procedure. We understand what he is doing when he does it. And this seems to be sufficient to give a use to statements about changes in the past, since we have specified possible situations in which at least this person might talk about such changes. And these situations have been specified without changing our conceptual system, for the "remains" that do not change in this way are still regarded as evidence about past events.

The sceptic claims that there could be changes in the

past and, hence, that historical propositions cannot be known to be true. To refute this form of scepticism, it is not enough to show that the expression " a change in the past" *does not* have a use, hence that this expression is meaningless, and hence that there are no changes in the past. If this expression *could* be given a use, then this expression could be meaningful and changes in the past *could* occur. The sceptic would thus be refuted only by showing that this expression *could not* be given a use. But, as shown above, apparently it could be given a use, and so, apparently, changes in the past could occur. The possibility of changes in the past gives strong support to the sceptic's thesis that historical propositions cannot be known to be true.

PART

V

In Parts I and II I gave particular and detailed examples of two theories, which I call "Construction Theories of History." It is clear that these theories deal with fundamental problems in the philosophy of history and deserve considerable attention, even though they may ultimately be found to be unsatisfactory. In Parts III and IV I considered certain arguments for scepticism about the possibility of historical knowledge, these being primarily intended as arguments for the Constructionist position.

In Chapter Eleven I wish to consider three topics. In the first section I will state exactly how the arguments in Part IV, if sound, provide support for the Constructionist position. The second section concerns the general characteristics shared by every particular Constructionist theory. And in the third section I will try to show that a certain objection to the Construction Theory of History does not present that theory with a serious difficulty.

I have considered only one family of arguments for Constructionism, namely, those involving historical scepticism. I do not claim that these arguments conclusively prove the Constructionist thesis but, instead, that they give that thesis a certain amount of plausibility, thus showing that that thesis deserves serious consideration. The type of argument I have given for that thesis is undoubtedly not the only type of argument that can be given for it.

Hence, even if scepticism about historical knowledge is not ultimately justifiable, this would not show that Constructionism is unfounded, since there are very probably other sorts of arguments that can be given for it.

Finally, Constructionists do not deny that most, if not all, philosophers of history and historians hold the Discovery Theory of History. Constructionists are not trying to describe what views these people do *hold. They are trying to show that the Discovery Theory of History ought to be abandoned. They are trying to show that a certain view of history* ought *to be held, instead of the one now widely held.*

CHAPTER ELEVEN

𐃩𐃩𐃩𐃩𐃩𐃩𐃩𐃩𐃩

THE CONSTRUCTION THEORY
OF HISTORY

The Relation Between Scepticism
and Constructionist Theories of History

In Part IV I presented and discussed a number of arguments for scepticism about historical knowledge. I do not claim that such scepticism has thereby been proven correct. That is, I do not claim that any of the arguments discussed in Part IV have been proven to be ultimately sound. What I do claim is that they have been shown to be plausible—in certain cases, I believe, highly plausible. Each of these arguments may be ultimately unsound. For example, it may be possible to give an ultimate justification of the use of memory, to describe a satisfactory method for acquiring the concept of the past, and to exhibit a contradiction in the notion of a change in the past. But if any *one* of the arguments discussed in Part IV is ultimately sound, then historical knowledge is impossible (where "historical knowledge," of course, means "knowledge of some independent realm of past events obtained through the use of evidence"). The soundness of only one of these arguments will conclusively justify scepticism about historical knowledge.

Whether or not historical knowledge is possible is a very important problem in itself, and Parts III and IV of this book, taken by themselves, can be regarded as dealing with this problem by itself. But even more important is the relation between scepticism and the problem of the nature of history. If historical knowledge is impossible, this impossibility has serious consequences for theories of the nature of the historian's activities. Let us assume that one or more of the arguments given in Part IV is sound. What does this show about the nature of the historian's activities? I believe that this gives support to what I have called the "Construction Theory of History." Now I want to explain exactly how the soundness of one or more of the arguments for scepticism would provide support for this theory.

Historians typically regard themselves as probing a realm called "the past" and detecting events, institutions, trends, and so on that are lodged in that realm. To be sure, they admit they never directly confront past events, but they believe that proper use of present evidence will give reliable information about those events. If scepticism about historical knowledge is justified, it does not follow that historians cannot continue to be regarded as probing the past. Historians can still be regarded as trying to discover facts about the past, even if it is impossible for them to succeed in discovering such facts. In these circumstances historians would be regarded as trying to do something that is impossible. But it is certainly possible for someone to try to do the impossible. For example, in earlier centuries mathematicians tried to trisect an angle using only ruler and compasses, even though it was later proved that it is impossible to trisect an angle in this way. So if scepticism about historical knowledge is correct, it does not follow that the view that historians are trying to discover facts about the past is false.

It may be the case that if the historian himself comes to believe that it is impossible to discover facts about the past, he cannot regard himself, nor can we regard him, as trying to discover facts about the past. For it may be that a person cannot try to do that which he believes to be impossible, even though he can try to do what is impossible so long as he does not believe it to be impossible. But still, some historians—namely, those who do not believe it impossible to discover facts about the past—could still regard themselves as trying to discover facts about the past. So the soundness of scepticism about historical knowledge does not, by itself, show the Discovery Theory of History to be untenable in the sense of showing that historians and philosophers of history do not and cannot regard historians as trying to discover facts about the past.

But if any one of the arguments in Part IV is sound, and if we believe that history is an important and significant activity, we will have a very good reason to regard the Discovery Theory of History as unsatisfactory. For if it is impossible to discover facts about the past, the historian would, on the Discovery Theory of History, be trying to do what is impossible. And on what grounds could this attempt to do the impossible be regarded as important and significant? The Discovery Theory of History would be unsatisfactory because it would then show written history to be insignificant and unimportant. So the arguments for scepticism, if sound, do not show the Discovery Theory of History to be false as a description or possible description of what historians do. Instead, these arguments would show that theory to be unsatisfactory in the sense just explained. They would not show that one *could not* hold the Discovery Theory of History; they would show that one *ought not* to hold that theory of history.

However, it does not follow from the proposition that the Discovery Theory of History is unsatisfactory that the Construction Theory of History *is* satisfactory. This does not follow for two reasons: (1) The Construction Theory of History may not be the only alternative to the Discovery Theory of History; (2) there may be serious objections to the Constructionist position itself; that is, this theory may be itself unsatisfactory in various ways not having to do with scepticism. I will discuss one possible objection to the Constructionist position later in this chapter.

Thus, the arguments for scepticism, if sound, discredit the Discovery Theory of History. They do not discredit the Construction Theory of History in this way. If these two theories are the only possible theories of history—and it seems quite probable that they are—then these arguments, if sound, show that the Constructionist position ought to be adopted.

The Construction Theory of History

The expression "Construction Theory of History" is intended to apply to a class of particular theories of history. The members of this class share certain features in virtue of which they belong to the same class. The two main features of every particular Constructionist theory are: (1) a claim that the historian should not be regarded as trying to discover facts about an independently existing realm of past events; (2) a claim that history is nevertheless important and significant because it attempts to deal with a certain class of present entities (which we will call "documents" and which includes artifacts, memoirs, records, and memory beliefs) in a certain way. According to this second claim, the historian "tells a story" which is in the past tense. Each historian creates the past or a part of the past in writing history. In doing this, the historian is still doing something important, even if he is not detecting facts about the past; for he is trying to give a coherent account of presently existing objects (namely, the documents) which, as we say, are related to past events. He tells a story that accounts for the existence and nature of those documents. By giving an account of certain parts of the world—present documents, present institutions, and, in general, any part of the present world which, as we say, "indicates something about the past"—the historian helps, along with those working in other fields, to give a coherent account of the *present* world as a whole. This shows that, on the Constructionist view, the historian is doing something important.

How do historians deal with or account for documents, according to Constructionism? We must first distinguish between the general goal the historian is trying to achieve with respect to the documents and the methods he uses to achieve that goal. The theories of history we are discussing concern the historian's general goal. Thus both the Constructionist and the holder of the Discovery Theory of History could agree that historians ought to use certain methods, while disagreeing about the reasons why they should use those methods.

What should be the general goal of the historian, on the Constructionist position? Here, particular Constructionist theories will differ. According to Croce, historians attempt to construct accounts of the past that will "answer to" present interests. Some other Constructionist might say, as Oakeshott sometimes seems to say, that the historian's task is to construct an account or tell a story that would link together or establish relations between the documents or perhaps would be a plausible explanation of how the documents came to be as they are. For example, if we have two documents that seem to be records of the same event but differ from one another in certain ways, the historian might construct an account or tell a story (or, as I have put it, "create a part of the past") according to which one document was written immediately after the event by an eye-witness, whereas the other was written much later and based on hearsay. This would link the two documents by giving each a role in a story which is put in the past tense. Of course, this would not be an account of what historians do. For historians often do not mention in their accounts the documents on which those accounts are based. So this particular Constructionist theory would be revisionary in two ways: (1) it would urge that the historian's goal be construed in the way described above; (2) it would urge that the historian construct accounts that do explicitly show how the documents are related to one another in that account. But the Constructionist of this stripe would also say that these relations of the documents to one another are *already* implicit in the accounts historians now construct on the basis of those documents and that he is urging them only to make these relations among the documents an explicit feature of these accounts. So his theory would not be totally revisionary.

This Constructionist can say that the historian's accounts are or should be *about* the documents, even though the documents are in the present and the constructed account is in the past tense. But what description of the historian's account can be given by another type of Constructionist—namely, one who believes, on the basis of the arguments given in Chapters Eight and Nine, that propositions in the past tense are not meaningful and who believes that the historian's accounts should not be about the documents? This type of Constructionist (of which Oakeshott's position, as described in the next-to-last section of Chapter Two, is one example) cannot say that the historian's account is about the past, because he also claims that no one can understand what it is for a proposition to be about the past. Nor can he say that the historian's account is "as if it were about the past," for one cannot know what it is for something to be *as if it were* about the past unless he also knows what it is for something to *be* about the past. Even if this were a difficulty with this particular variety of Constructionism, it is not a difficulty with Constructionism in general, because other varieties of Constructionism can give a characterization of the historian's account. They can say that the accounts are about the documents or, in the case of those Constructionists who believe that we cannot have evidence about the past but who believe that past-tense propositions are meaningful, they can say that these accounts are "as if they were about the past" or that they are about a "supposed" past.

To describe the Constructionist position further would be to continue to describe particular Constructionist theories, because the only characteristics particular Constructionist theories have in common seem to be the two listed earlier. For example, two Constructionist views will agree that the historian should not be regarded as detecting facts about an independent past. But they may disagree as to how the past is to be viewed by the historian. One may hold that there is no such thing as the past and that this is why the historian is not concerned with the past; the other may claim that there is a past, but that the historian is not concerned with it for some other reason. Again, two particular theories may disagree on what principles the historian should use in constructing parts of the past. One may claim that the historian should use exactly the principles he now uses. The other may claim that he should use new principles, for example, that the historian should not be concerned about bias, perhaps for the reasons given in Chapter Five (pp. 103–110), and should allow his standards and values to influence his constructions of parts of the past more than they now do. Again, we have seen that Constructionists may differ over the purpose of constructing parts of the past and over what the historian's accounts are about. They may also disagree about the criteria of evaluation of written histories. An example of one such criterion will be given in the next section.

The arguments for the Constructionist theory considered in this book are arguments only for the general position and do not support one particular Constructionist theory over another. These are arguments for the first feature of Constructionism, namely, that the historian should not be regarded as detecting facts about the past. All particular Constructionist theories assent to this principle. Hence, all particular Constructionist theories are equally supported by this type of argument. It might be said that there could be a theory of history which also assented to this first principle but which was a non-Constructionist theory in that it did not assent to the second principle. And this non-Constructionist theory would also be supported by this argument. It is perhaps logically possible that there be such a non-Constructionist position. But if it did try to show that the historian was doing something meaningful and important, what principle could such a non-Constructionist theory put forth in place of the second principle of Constructionism?

An Objection to the Construction Theory of History

Some will feel that the Construction Theory is not only extremely paradoxical (which it is) but also very implausible and even, perhaps, obviously unsatisfactory. But such a belief can be supported only by a refutation of each argument supporting the theory or the setting forth of serious objections to the Constructionist view itself. And such an opinion of the Constructionist view must be supported in one or both of these ways if it is to have any weight. In Part IV I discussed objections of the first type to Constructionism, namely, various objections to each of the arguments for scepticism. In this section I wish to discuss an objection of the second kind mentioned above, namely, an ostensible difficulty with the Constructionist theory itself.

Every theory of history tries to take into account all or most of the distinctions that are usually made in the philosophy of history—for instance, those between fact and interpretation and between history and chronicle (see the introduction to Chapter One). The objection to Constructionism I wish to discuss here concerns another distinction, namely, that between history itself and historical fiction. According to this objection, there is no difference between the two on the Constructionist view. But there is, in fact, a difference between the two. Therefore the Constructionist view is not adequate.

Why is it said that the Constructionist view cannot account for the difference between history and historical fiction? The objector would allege that history differs from historical fiction in that written history corresponds to the facts, or at least is intended to do so, whereas much of historical fiction is purely imaginary and is not intended to correspond to the facts. But on the Constructionist view, written history itself is not viewed as corresponding to past events. Written history is just a story, as a historical novel is. Hence there is no difference between the two on this theory.

But the primary difference between history and historical fiction is not that history is intended to correspond to the facts, whereas historical fiction is not. After all, a writer of historical fiction could *intend* that his work completely correspond to the facts, but this would not make it any less a work of historical fiction or more a work of history. Nor would his work be any more of a history if it did in fact *happen* to correspond to the facts. Furthermore, the difference between the two is not basically a difference of form. Most written histories do not contain dialogue between historical figures, but they could do so and still be histories rather than historical fiction. For even if there was no evidence that any such dialogue occurred in the past, the historian could use such dialogue to help to convey his interpretation of the era he is concerned with. So long as it was noted by the historian that this was the function of dialogue in his work, his work would not cease to be history just because it contained dialogue, as historical fiction does. (A well-known example of this use of dialogue by a historian is the Melian dialogue in Thucydides' *History of the Peloponnesian War*.) And, in fact, if the dialogue of historical fiction is viewed in this way—as presenting an interpretation of the events in question—probably some works presently classified as historical fiction would come to be regarded as histories. None of the differences so far mentioned is the basic difference between history and historical fiction. Instead, the basic difference is that written history is largely if not entirely based on documents, whereas much of historical fiction has no basis at all in the documents.

Given that this is the difference between history and historical fiction, I believe that this difference can be accounted for by at least some Constructionist theories. Let us consider this question in relation to the variety of Constructionism which holds that the historian's task is to link the documents. If the work contains parts that have little or nothing to do with the evidence or documents, as works of historical fiction do, then those parts are not essential for the linking of documents. And there is probably a way of linking the documents or explaining their existence that does not include those parts which have little or nothing to do with the documents. So this variety of Constructionism can include a principle (which some allege that the sciences use) according to which written histories are evaluated partly on the basis of whether they contain parts not necessary for the linking and explaining of documents. Any work that does include such parts may be labelled "historical fiction." Of course, such a work may not have the form—dialogue and other facets—usually associated with historical fiction; it may, in fact, have exactly the same form acceptable histories have. But we have seen that form is not an essential characteristic of historical fiction in any case, and that historical fiction cannot be distinguished from history by its form.

In view of this, I believe that the objection concerning the difference between history and historical fiction is not a serious objection to the Construction Theory of History. For the Constructionist position can account for the difference between the two.

Conclusion

I have tried to show that the Construction Theory of History is deserving of serious consideration and examination. I do not claim that I have proved it to be correct or even that it will ultimately turn out to be sound. But I do claim to have shown that it can be defended and given a considerable measure of plausibility in the ways indicated in Parts IV and V. Interpretations of Croce's and Oakeshott's views have been given as particular examples of Constructionist theories. But I have been defending the general Constructionist position, and even if their theories are not ultimately defensible, this general position may still be satisfactory. This general position and the particular theories are worthy of considerable discussion because they are concerned with some of the most important problems in the philosophy of history.

NOTES

All references labelled "G" are to excerpts from the works in question in Patrick Gardiner's THEORIES OF HISTORY *(New York: Free Press of Glencoe, 1959).*

CHAPTER ONE

1. W. H. Walsh, *An Introduction to the Philosophy of History* (London: Hutchinson & Co., Ltd., 1958), pp. 13, 42, 56.
2. Benedetto Croce, *History: Its Theory and Practice* (New York: Russell & Russell, Inc., 1960), quoted by permission of Russell & Russell, Inc. Also published as *Theory and History of Historiography* (London: George G. Harrap & Co., Ltd., 1921). The interpretation I give of Croce's theory of history is of that theory as presented in this work. All subsequent references in Chapter One are to this work.
3. p. 51.
4. pp. 12–13; G, pp. 227–228.
5. p. 12; G, p. 227.
6. p. 19; G, p. 231.
7. pp. 24–25; G, p. 232.
8. p. 12; G, p. 227.
9. p. 12; G, p. 227.
10. p. 73; G, p. 239.
11. p. 73; G, p. 239.
12. p. 75; G, p. 240.
13. p. 111.
14. p. 110.
15. p. 112.
16. p. 112.
17. p. 110.
18. p. 108.
19. pp. 109–110.
20. p. 14; G, p. 228.
21. p. 14; G, p. 228.
22. p. 27.
23. p. 33.
24. pp. 35–36.
25. p. 37.
26. p. 64; G, p. 234.
27. p. 65; G, p. 234.
28. p. 115.
29. p. 115.
30. p. 76; G, p. 240.
31. p. 57.
32. p. 30.
33. p. 109.
34. p. 54.
35. p. 15; G, p. 228.
36. p. 31.
37. p. 139.
38. p. 33.
39. p. 136.

CHAPTER TWO

1. Michael Oakeshott, *Experience and Its Modes* (Cambridge, Eng.: Cambridge University Press, 1933), quoted with permission of the author, pp. 109–110. All subsequent references in this chapter are to this work unless otherwise indicated.
2. p. 92.
3. p. 93.
4. p. 93.
5. p. 93.
6. p. 13.
7. p. 95.
8. p. 108.
9. p. 103.
10. p. 107.
11. p. 107.
12. p. 108.
13. p. 108.
14. p. 108.
15. p. 113.
16. p. 100.
17. p. 42.
18. pp. 104–105.
19. p. 119.
20. p. 118.
21. p. 118.
22. p. 125.
23. p. 124.
24. p. 124.
25. Walsh, *An Introduction to the Philosophy of History*, p. 89.
26. pp. 146–147.

CHAPTER THREE

1. R. G. Collingwood, *The Idea of History* (Oxford: The Clarendon Press, 1946), quoted by permission of the Clarendon Press, Oxford, p. 158. All subsequent references in this chapter are to this work unless otherwise indicated.
2. p. 214; G, p. 252.
3. A different but in some respects similar explanation of this dictum is given by P. H. Nowell-Smith in "Are Historical Events Unique?", *Proceedings of the Aristotelian Society* LVII (1956–57), 145.
4. p. 213.
5. pp. 284–285.
6. pp. 285–286.
7. p. 286.
8. p. 286.
9. p. 288.
10. Alan Donagan, *The Later Philosophy of R. G. Collingwood* (Oxford: Oxford University Press, 1962), p. 221.
11. p. 287.
12. Croce, *History: Its Theory and Practice*, pp. 134–135; G, p. 233.

CHAPTER FOUR

1. J. C. Holt, *King John* (London: The Historical Association, 1963). I wish to thank J. T. Rosenthal for suggesting this reference.
2. Holt, p. 5.
3. Croce, *History: Its Theory and Practice*, p. 36.
4. Ernest Nagel, "Some Issues in the Logic of Historical Analysis," *Scientific Monthly* LXXIV (1952), 166; G, p. 380.
5. Nagel, p. 167; G, p. 381.

Also Ernest Nagel, *The Structure of Science* (New York and Burlingame: Harcourt, Brace and World, Inc., 1961), p. 500.
6. Isaiah Berlin, *Historical Inevitability* (Oxford: Oxford University Press, 1954), pp. 59, 65–66; G, pp. 324, 328.
7. Second-Level Relativism is mentioned by Berlin on p. 48 of *Historical Inevitability*.

CHAPTER SEVEN

1. C. I. Lewis, *An Analysis of Knowledge and Valuation* (La Salle, Ill.: Open Court Publishing Co., 1946), p. 334.
2. See Chapter Nine (pp. 168–170) for further discussion of the possibility of observing the past.
3. Lewis, p. 354.
4. Lewis, p. 339.
5. Lewis, p. 341.
6. Lewis, p. 338.
7. Lewis, p. 345.

CHAPTER NINE

1. Philip Wiener (ed.), *Leibniz: Selections* (New York: Charles Scribner's Sons, 1951), p. 287.
2. Wiener, pp. 286–287.
3. Edward J. Bond, "The Concept of the Past," *Mind* LXXII (1963), 533–544.
4. Bond, p. 544.
5. Bond, p. 544.
6. Bond, p. 544.

7. A. D. Woozley, *Theory of Knowledge* (London: Hutchinson & Co., 1949), p. 49.
8. Woozley, p. 49.
9. Woozley, p. 49.
10. A. J. Ayer presents a similar view in *The Problem of Knowledge* (London: Macmillan and Co., Ltd., 1956), Chapter Four.

CHAPTER TEN

1. C. D. Broad, *The Mind and Its Place in Nature* (London: Kegan Paul, Trench, Trubner & Co., Ltd., 1925), pp. 251–252.

2. G. E. M. Anscombe, "The Reality of the Past" in Max Black (ed.), *Philosophical Analysis* (Englewood Cliffs, N. J.: Prentice-Hall, 1963), p. 48.

3. Anscombe, pp. 51–52.

4. Anscombe, p. 51.

SELECTED BIBLIOGRAPHY

Items 4, 5, 10, 11, and 18 are found either in whole or in part in Patrick Gardiner (ed.), THEORIES OF HISTORY *(New York: Free Press of Glencoe, 1959).*

1. G. E. M. ANSCOMBE, "The Reality of the Past" in Max Black (ed.), *Philosophical Analysis* (Englewood Cliffs, N. J.: Prentice-Hall, 1963).

2. A. J. AYER, *The Problem of Knowledge* (London: Macmillan and Co., Ltd., 1956), Chapter 4.

3. A. J. AYER, "Statements about the Past" in *Philosophical Essays* (London: Macmillan and Co., Ltd., 1954).

4. ISAIAH BERLIN, *Historical Inevitability* (Oxford: Oxford University Press, 1954).

5. C. BLAKE, "Can History Be Objective?" *Mind* **LXIV** (1955), 61–78.

6. EDWARD J. BOND, "The Concept of the Past," *Mind* **LXXII** (1963), 533–544.

7. RICHARD B. BRANDT, "The Epistemological Status of Memory Beliefs," *Philosophical Review* **LXIV** (1955), 78–95.

8. C. D. BROAD, *Examination of McTaggart's Philosophy* (Cambridge, Eng.: Cambridge University Press, 1933–38), Volume II.

9. C. D. BROAD, *The Mind and Its Place in Nature* (London: Kegan Paul, Trench, Trubner & Co., Ltd., 1925).

10. R. G. COLLINGWOOD, *The Idea of History* (Oxford: The Clarendon Press, 1946). Collingwood discusses Croce and Oakeshott, among others, in the first part of this work and presents his own theory of history in the second part. Available in a paperback edition.

11. BENEDETTO CROCE, *History: Its Theory and Practice* (New York: Russell & Russell, Inc., 1960).

12. ALAN DONAGAN, *The Later Philosophy of R. G. Collingwood* (Oxford: Oxford University Press, 1962).

13. C. I. LEWIS, *An Analysis of Knowledge and Valuation* (LaSalle, Ill.: Open Court Publishing Co., 1946), Chapter XI.

14. NORMAN MALCOLM, "Memory and the Past" in *Knowledge and Certainty* (Englewood Cliffs, N. J.: Prentice-Hall, 1963).

15. M. MANDELBAUM, *The Problem of Historical Knowledge* (New York: Liveright Publishing Corp., 1938).

16. W. R. MATTHEWS, "What Is an Historical Event?" *Proceedings of the Aristotelian Society* **XXXVIII** (1937–38), 207–216.

17. GEORGE HERBERT MEAD, *The Philosophy of the Present* (LaSalle, Ill.: Open Court Publishing Co., 1932), Chapter I.

18. ERNEST NAGEL, "Some Issues in the Logic of Historical Analysis," *Scientific Monthly* **LXXIV** (1952), 162–169.

19. ERNEST NAGEL, *The Structure of Science* (New York and Burlingame: Harcourt, Brace and World, Inc., 1961).

20. J. O. NELSON, "The Validation of Memory and Our Conception of a Past," *Philosophical Review* **LXXII** (1963), 35–47.

21. P. H. NOWELL-SMITH, "Are Historical Events Unique?" *Proceedings of the Aristotelian Society* **LVII** (1956–57), 107–160.

22. H. D. OAKELEY, "The Status of the Past," *Proceedings of the Aristotelian Society* **XXXII** (1931–32), 227–250.

23. MICHAEL OAKESHOTT, *Experience and Its Modes* (Cambridge, Eng.: Cambridge University Press, 1933), Chapter 3.

24. RICHARD TAYLOR, "The 'Justification' of Memories and the Analogy of Vision," *Philosophical Review* **LXV** (1956), 192–205.

25. W. H. WALSH, *An Introduction to the Philosophy of History* (London: Hutchinson & Co., Ltd., 1958), Chapters 4 and 5.

26. A. D. WOOZLEY, *Theory of Knowledge* (London: Hutchinson & Co., Ltd., 1949), Chapters 2 and 3.

INDEX

Acts of thought: Collingwood on, 69–82; enactments of, 78–81; exact similarity of, 70–81; numerical identity of, 70–81; relation to time, 80–81

Analogy, the argument from, 118–119

Anscombe, G. E. M., 180–186

Berlin, Isaiah, 92–99

Bias in history, 86ff.

Bond, Edward J., 162–168

Broad, C. D., 174, 178

"Brute facts," 88; Croce's denial of, 20–22, 26–27; Oakeshott on, 52–53, 54

Changes in the past, 57–58; Anscombe on the possibility of, 180–185; meaningfulness of statements about, 180–186; possibility of, 180–186; and scepticism, 177–179, 185–186; types of, 175–177

Chronicle, Croce on, 17–18

Coherence, 51–53; of memory beliefs, 128–135

Collingwood, R. G., 28, 63ff.; on actions, 68; on acts of thought, see Acts of thought; and Constructionism, 82; and Croce, 81; Donagan on, 78–79; and evidence, 64; on intentions, 64–69; on the past as brought into the

present, 63ff.; on reenactment, 64, 65, 69–82; and scepticism, 63–65, 81–82

Concept of the past, 57, 156–172, 173–177; memory and, 160–161, 163–168; scepticism and, 172

Congruence and memory beliefs, 130–135

Constructionism, v, 3, 4, 7, 8; and Collingwood, 82; and Croce, 14, 15, 16, 32–38; features of, 192–196; and the justification of memory beliefs, 121–141; and Oakeshott, 55, 62; relation to scepticism, 6–7, 8, 189–192; and relativism, 110

Contemporary history: Croce on, 16–17; Oakeshott on, 41–49

Correlation Argument, the, 113–120, 140

Croce, Benedetto, v, 7, 8, 13ff., 42, 48, 52, 54, 62, 81, 87, 110, 193; "brute facts," 20–22, 26–27; on chronicle, 17–18; and Constructionism, 14, 15, 16, 32–38; on contemporary history and past history, 16–17; deterministic history, 26; documents, 22–23; evidence, 21; facts, 19–22, 29–31; historical and non-historical facts, 22–23; and Idealism, 13; interests,

16, 18–24, 29–32; on interpretations, 19–22, 29–31; on periodization, 27; philological history, 24–25; poetical history, 25–26; rejection of other theories of history, 24–31; and relativism, 14, 20, 35–37, 110; on revivals, 18; teleological history, 26–27

Deterministic history, Croce on, 26
Discovery Theory of History, the, 4, 14, 190–192
Documents, Croce on the preservation of, 22–23
Donagan, Alan, 78–79

Ether, the, 43
Events, essential properties of, 147–149
Evidence, 21, 48–49, 56–60, 64, 113–120, 185

Facts: Croce on, 19–23, 29–31; historical and non-historical, 22–23
First-Level Relativism, 85–88, 101–102, 109–110

Gödel, K., 6

Hegel, G. W. F., 19
Historical fiction: Constructionism on, 196–198
Historical knowledge, possibility of, *see* Scepticism
Holt, J. C., 86

Idealism, v, 3, 7, 13, 41
Interests, 16, 18–24, 29–32
Interpretation, historical, 52; Croce on, 19–22, 29–31; and relativism, 86ff.

Judgments, 43–48, 85–110; agreement in historical judgments, 104–110

Leibniz, G. W. F., 157–158, 159
Lewis, C. I., 124–125, 130–135

Mead, G. H., 7–8
Memory beliefs: certainty about some memory beliefs, 135–139; and Constructionism, 141; the justification of, 120, 121–141; and personal identity, 138, 146; and scepticism, 140–141

Nagel, Ernest, 89–92

Oakeshott, Michael, v, 7, 8, 28, 41ff., 63–64, 193, 194; on "brute facts," 52–53; changes in the past, 57–58; coherence, 51–53; concept of the past, 57; and Constructionism, 55, 62; evidence, 48–49, 56–57; history as contemporary, 41–49; on judgments, 43–48; meaning of statements about the past, 50–51, 57–60; on objects, 43–48; on past events, 41–49; postulates of history, 54–55; relation between past and present, 50–51, 55, 59–60; and scepticism, 48–49, 51, 60–62; on sensations, 44–46; Walsh on, 56
Objectivity, 92–98, 103–110
Objects, 43–48

Past events, 13ff., 41–49, 174; relation between past and, 173–177; relation between present and, 50–51, 55, 59–60, 160–161, 171–172

Periodization, Croce on, 27

Personal identity, and memory beliefs, 138, 146

Philological history, 24–25

Poetical history, 25–26

Reality of the past, scepticism about, 41ff., 127

Relativism, historical, 85–110; and agreement in historical judgments, 104–110; Berlin on, 92–99; and Constructionism, 110; and Croce, 14, 20, 35–37, 110; First-Level, 85–88, 101–102, 109–110; Nagel on, 89–92; objectivity, 92–98, 103, 110; refutation of, 103–110; Relativist's claim, 85–88, 108; Second-Level, 88, 99, 101–103, 109–110; standards and values in history, influence of, 85–88, 105–109

Revivals, 18

Scepticism, historical, v, 4–6; and changes in the past, 177–179, 185–186; and Collingwood, 63–65, 81–82; and the concept of the past, 172; and Croce, 14, 25, 32–38; and the justification of memory beliefs, 121–141; and Oakeshott, 48–49, 60–62; relation to Constructionism, 6–7, 8, 189–192

Second-Level Relativism, 88, 99, 101–103, 109–110

Sensations, Oakeshott on, 44–46

Specious present, the, 168–170

Standards and values, influence on historical judgments, 85–88, 105–109

Statements about the past: conditions of meaningfulness of, 142–145, 155–159; conditions of truth of, 178–179; content of, 152–154; meaning of, 50–51, 57–60

Teleological history, 26–27

Time travel, 114–115, 116, 145

Verbs: past tense, use of, 161–168; tensed and tenseless, 152–154

Verification Argument, the, 142–154

Walsh, W. H., 56

Woozley, A. D., 169–170